EASTERN EDITION

# Common Birds
## *of* North America

## AN EXPANDED GUIDEBOOK

James D. Wilson

Willow Creek®
PRESS

# MAP KEY

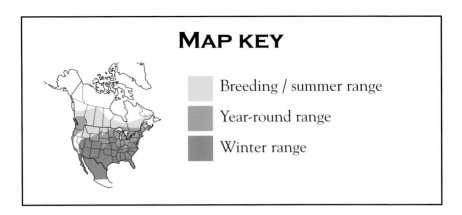

Breeding / summer range

Year-round range

Winter range

Published by Willow Creek Press, P.O. Box 147, Minocqua, Wisconsin 54548

Design by Patricia Bickner Linder
Edited by Andrea Donner

For information on other Willow Creek Press titles, call 1-800-850-9453

Library of Congress Cataloging-in-Publication Data
   Wilson, James D.
      Common birds of North America : an expanded guidebook / by James D. Wilson.-- Eastern edition.
         p.  cm.
      ISBN 1-57223-313-3 (softcover : alk. paper)
      1. Birds--East (U.S.)--Identification.  I. Title.
      QL683.E27  W55  2001
      598'.07'23474--dc21

                                                    2001003683


Printed in Canada

*To Marsha, Christopher, and Corey*

# CONTENTS

# INTRODUCTION

irds are our most conspicuous wildlife. They are active; many are brightly-colored with beautiful voices; and they are right out there for us to see, enjoy, and learn about — on fence wires, in treetops, over our heads, on our lawns, and as close as our bird feeders. It is quite natural that there is such interest in them. Most bird enthusiasts are not avid chasers of unusual bird species. They simply want to know the identity and something about the birds that they see around their homes, flitting outside their office windows, or flying overhead as they are stopped at a traffic light. Throughout my 24 years as a professional ornithologist, people have contacted me regularly with their questions and observations about the common birds they see on a regular basis. These are the people for whom this book is written.

This book addresses most questions about Eastern birds by focusing on only the 90 most common species. By not including the birds that are less likely to be seen, the text can cover in detail the birds that are included, helping with identification and informing the reader about the particulars of the birds' biology. These 90 species represent at least 98 percent of the birds that a person in the northeastern states is likely to see. Though a few birds in this book may be less known, all are common enough that one can become familiar with them with little effort. The key to seeing these birds is to watch birds in all seasons and to be aware of them wherever you are — at home, on walks through the park, and on drives through the countryside.

Each species is presented with a color illustration and an associated narrative. Most of the illustrations are simple portraits showing birds behaving as expected and in habitat typical for that species. These life-like portrayals are meant to impart identification cues, in addition to color and shape. They are also intended to inform visually about that bird's life history as they sometimes show nests, eggs, foods, and feeding behavior. Birds usually seen in the sky are shown from below. Those that perch in trees, bushes, or on the ground, are depicted with an example of the cover in which they might be found.

The narratives accompanying each illustration begin with a description of the species' physical characteristics, including those sexual and seasonal variations that are not depicted in the illustrations. They proceed to describe the bird's sound, habitat, feeding behavior, winter and summer ranges, and the dates of migration. For those that nest in the East, the narratives conclude with a discussion of courtship behavior, nest location, color and number of eggs, and the length of time required for incubation and rearing. In some cases, human relationships to the featured bird are mentioned, such as methods of feeding, placement of nest boxes, or those that have been selected as State Birds.

The region covered — the East — for the purposes of this book, includes Washington DC plus the 13 most northeastern states: New York,

New Jersey, Connecticut, Rhode Island, Massachusetts, Vermont, New Hampshire, Maine, Pennsylvania, Delaware, Maryland, Virginia, West Virginia; and eastern provinces of Canada. Some of the birds featured are more common in certain portions of the region than others. A few, though numerous in certain locales, were not included if absent form the majority of the region. However, despite the large size of this geographical area, most of the birds featured are common throughout.

The arrangement of the birds in this book is standard with a few exceptions. It is based on a professional classification scheme that places closely related species together. Other bird literature is likely to cover them in the same sequence. Though this arrangement may seem confusing at first, it should be easy to find a bird of interest, because of the relatively few birds covered in this book. A hint to success is to realize that the first 36 species include such diverse groups as waterfowl, large birds of prey, hummingbirds, and woodpeckers. The last 54 species are classified as songbirds or perching birds, beginning with the aerial insectivores and ending with those that have heavier bills for cracking seed coats. Two exceptions to this arrangement are the American Crow and American Tree Sparrow, which are songbirds placed in the first one-third of the book as part of compositions.

I had great fun painting these birds in the postures and habitats in which I have seen them on hundreds of occasions. It is hoped that they occasionally illicit an "Aha, that's just the way I saw it" response when you compare a sighting to my portrayal. With little effort, all of these birds can be seen and enjoyed. Birds are a diverse group, composed of truly unique and fascinating species. The bird facts that I have presented will, hopefully, help you to appreciate your feathered neighbors all the more.

# HINTS FOR ENJOYING BIRDS

o get the most out of this book, be attentive to the birds wherever you are. Even when visual identification is not conclusive, many of the birds in this book can be identified from their behavior, the habitat where you see them, or by what season of the year it is. Some, however, may require careful examination. Binoculars help in seeing details; use them to look for certain features before turning to the book as the bird may not remain in view for long. In addition to color, remember whether the bird has an eye-line, wing-bars, or a plain or streaked breast. Light spots on the tail characterize certain warblers, and leg and bill color can be useful in clarifying which sparrow or warbler has been seen.

Although some species of birds can be seen nearly everywhere, many are only associated with a particular kind of habitat. For example, Brown Thrashers live in brushy thickets, Eastern Meadowlarks reside in grassland, and Scarlet Tanagers are associated with the woods. Therefore, to see the variety presented in this book, be aware of birds when in a variety of places. Likewise, habitat can be an identification cue. A small blue bird in a forest edge would more likely be an Indigo Bunting than an Eastern Bluebird. Similarly, season of the year can provide a clue to identification. American Tree Sparrows, for example, are not expected here in summer, so if a bird resembling one is seen in July, it is probably the similar-appearing Chipping Sparrow. A large part of successful bird identification is realizing what to expect, when and where.

Although we regularly hear birds sing and call, relatively few people are able to identify them by voice. Users of this book are encouraged to try to see the bird that is vocalizing so as to make a connection between the song that is described and the singer's actual identify. When auditory and visual identification concur, the learning of songs can begin to take place. Once tuned in to identifying birds by their voices, a new level of enjoyment can be achieved.

People who invite birds to their yards with feeders and nest boxes have an advantage in getting to know them. Sunflower seed, either in the shell or hulled, is most effective in attracting a diversity of delightful seed-eaters, including cardinals, chickadees, nuthatches, woodpeckers, and various finches. Juncos and sparrows that feed on the ground favor white-proso millet. Niger, or "thistle seed," though expensive, can be targeted to finches by using tubular, hanging feeders. Suet, or fat trimmings, attracts clinging birds such as woodpeckers, chickadees, and nuthatches; it can be provided for the birds by hanging a mesh bag on a tree limb.

Most people provide bird feeding stations only in winter, when birds seem especially willing to accept hand-outs. Summertime feeding is becoming increasingly popular, however, because of the variety of birds that are visiting at that season, many in their brightest plumage of the year. Summer customers might include such brilliant seed-eaters as Indigo Buntings, Rose-breasted Grosbeaks, and American Goldfinches. The warm period of the year is also the time to invite hummingbirds and orioles with special feeders filled with a "nectar." Early spring is the time to put up nest boxes for the dozen or more species in this book that might use them. People who put up houses or search out nests are most likely to see the eggs, young, and the parental behaviors described in this book.

If your interest in birds extends beyond those covered in this book, there are numerous field guides on the market that address the identification of thousands of birds in all color phases and in all regions of the country and world. But realize that these primarily cover details relating to identification. There are few books, other than this one, that provide life history plus identification details on an extensive list of common birds within a particular region of the country.

# ATTRACTING BIRDS TO FEEDERS

| SPECIES | FAVORITE FOODS | NOTES |
|---------|----------------|-------|
| Mourning Dove | Cracked corn, Millet | Feeds on ground |
| Woodpeckers | Suet, Sunflower | Can cling to feed |
| Blue Jay | Sunflower, Corn | Avoids swinging feeders |
| Tufted Titmouse | Whole sunflower | Hanging feeder |
| Chickadee | Hulled sunflower | Can cling to feed |
| Nuthatch | Sunflower, Peanut butter | Latter smeared on bark |
| Starling | Suet, Table scraps | Feeds in flocks |
| Eastern Towhee | Sunflower, Millet | Summering bird |
| White-crowned Sparrow | Hulled sunflower, Peanut hearts | Feeds on ground |
| White-throated Sparrow | Hulled Sunflower, Millet | Feeds on ground |
| Dark-eyed Junco | Millet | Feeds on ground |
| Northern Cardinal | Sunflower, Safflower | Feeds from a perch |
| Rose-breasted Grosbeak | Sunflower | Summering bird |
| Indigo Bunting | Millet | Summering bird |
| Purple/House Finch | Niger seed, Sunflower | Feeds in flocks |
| Goldfinch/Siskin | Niger seed, Millet, Sunflower | Feeders with small perches |
| House Sparrow | Bread crumbs, Millet | Feeds in flocks |
| Hummingbird/Oriole | Nectar (1 part sugar to 4 water) | Specific feeder styles |
| Mockingbird/Catbird | Jelly, Cut-up fruit | Placed on board, Summer |

**IDENTIFICATION TIPS**

▶ large size and blue-gray color overall; adults have a white coloration around their heads; underparts are darker

▶ their call is a series of deep hoarse croaks

# GREAT BLUE HERON
*Ardea herodias*

**N**orth America's largest herons stand three feet tall and have wings spanning six feet. Their broad wings beat in a deep, slow cadence that attests to their size, while their legs trail out behind. Except when just landing and taking off, their heads are folded back on their necks in an S shape, a posture that distinguishes them from cranes. Great Blue Herons are sometimes erroneously called cranes; however, the only cranes in North America are much less common.

Great Blue Herons are usually encountered while they are standing statuesquely in the shallows of a stream or lake, waiting for a fish to swim within striking range. Quarry, which can also include frogs and even field mice, is taken with surprising swiftness. After being speared, fish are juggled around to be swallowed headfirst so that spines do not impede the process. Amazingly large fish can sometimes be seen moving down a heron's throat as the bird retches.

Great Blue Herons winter in southern states and along the East Coast as far north as Massachusetts. They breed throughout the United States, typically in dense colonies that in some instances have used the same nest trees for decades. A colony still present near Plymouth, Massachusetts, was noted by the Pilgrims in 1620. Great Blue Herons return to the nesting colonies just after ice-breakup.

After seeing them as solitary hunters, it is surprising to witness how social they become at nest sites. Their two- to three-foot-wide stick nests are closely spaced through the spreading crowns of a few huge trees. At each, a courting pair fans the filamentous plumes on their heads, necks, and backs. As nest refurbishing gets underway, each nesting pair croaks, squawks, and spars viciously with their neighbors. Despite apparent havoc, the mutual protection offered by the colony lessens nest raiding by Blue Jays and American Crows.

Incubation of their three to six pale-blue eggs takes place in March, usually before the trees begin to leaf out. The parents take turns sitting on the eggs during the month-long incubation period. Both parents feed the chicks partially-digested fish during April through June as the young birds grow in the nest. Frightened chicks sometimes regurgitate this gruel onto people who have the misfortune of wandering in beneath the colony.

Following nesting, Great Blue Herons scatter across the countryside to fish in streams, marshes, ponds, and coastal estuaries. They are sometimes joined at these areas by Great Egrets (*Ardea alba*), waders of similar size and shape whose feathers are pure white.

**IDENTIFICATION TIPS**

▶ soars in wide circles, with wings in a shallow V

▶ when overhead, the blackish wings are of two tones (the flight feathers are paler)

▶ while soaring, they will often rock and tilt unsteadily

▶ their naked heads are relatively small.

▶ eagles have larger heads, shorter tails, and their wings lay flat when soaring

# TURKEY VULTURE

*Cathartes aura*

ommonly called "buzzards," these impressive birds are usually seen wheeling lazily overhead. Where one is seen, there are usually others scattered through the sky, apparently relying on each other to find food. Their wings span six feet, as compared to a Red-tailed Hawk's four, and they are held in a distinctive shallow V shape. Turkey Vultures are further distinguished by their black plumage, except for their silvery underwing. Turkey Vultures fly so effortlessly that they are able to spend hours simply gliding aloft, especially during the warmest part of the day when updraft and thermals provide them the greatest lift. On the rare occasions that they do flap their wings, the beats are surprisingly deep and slow.

Although Turkey Vultures are usually high in the sky, they sometimes swoop low over the land while tilting rapidly from side to side to maintain stability. This enables them to use odor in addition to vision in locating carrion. Unlike most birds, vultures have an excellent sense of smell as evidenced by their large nostrils and the over-sized olfactory lobes of their brains. Hungry vultures are sometimes misled by the smell of mushrooms and stagnant water. Natural gas companies have used circling vultures to locate leaks in pipelines.

Today's landscape and the prevalence of road kills apparently favor Turkey Vultures, as they remain common. Their food habits provide a purifying service as they remove diseased carcasses from the landscape. They are adapted for this lifestyle by being immune to diseases such as Salmonellosis and Botulism. Their bare heads reduce contamination of decaying material. It is the bare head that resulted in their common name, as in this way they resemble Wild Turkeys.

Turkey Vultures winter in southern states and migrate in March to occupy all but the most northern of the United States. Eggs are laid in March, typically in dark places such as shelter caves, hollow logs, stumps, and abandoned buildings. Incubation of their one to three white eggs requires about one month. Although adults are voiceless, nestlings are able to hiss. When frightened, they also vomit through their nostrils, a sight and smell no doubt discouraging to many would-be predators. At the age of two to three months, the adult-sized young reluctantly leave the nest. Non-nesting Turkey Vultures often roost together at night in large trees in sheltered valleys. They migrate south in September.

# CANADA GOOSE

*Branta canadensis*

onsidering the regularity with which we now see Canada Geese, it is remarkable to realize that they did not even breed in the East until early in the 1900s. At one time, they were the mysterious "honkers" seen overhead en route to some far off land. Now, throughout much of the country, they flock like noisy poultry along lakes in parks and on golf courses. It is the combination of water and mown lawns that attracts Canada Geese, as they are one of few birds able to digest cellulose-rich material such as grass. Like their mammalian counterparts, cattle, they must graze almost constantly to derive their needed nutrition.

Though increasingly familiar, Canada Geese remain impressive. Those individuals that remain year-round to nest in the East are "Giant" Canada Geese, a race in which the males, or ganders, can weigh nearly 20 pounds and have a wingspan of six feet. Females are slightly smaller. Native to the Midwest, "Giants" were brought from the brink of extinction with the placement of nesting tubs in ponds, and by releases throughout the country. "Interior" Canada Geese, another race of the species, winter in large flocks from the Chesapeake Bay southward through the Carolinas. They are one-third smaller than "Giants" and remain the "wild goose" of lore, flying over us to nest in extreme northern Canada.

Flocks typically fly in V formations while emitting deep two-syllabled *hu-onks*. Male-female bonds are permanent, and the pair often travels with young from the previous year until ready to nest the following spring. The female constructs a nest lined with down from her own breast and commonly lays five to six cream-colored eggs. Resident "Giant" Canada Geese lay eggs as early as March. Once incubation begins, the goose rarely leaves her nest for the 25 to 28 days required for the young to hatch. The gander stands guard and courageously attacks any creature he perceives as a threat. Newly-hatched young are precocial, which means that they are covered with down and able to follow their parents and feed soon after hatching. They grow quickly, and are able to fly by mid-summer.

## IDENTIFICATION TIPS

▶ in flight, the white belly contrasts with the dark breast and wings

▶ long square tail, short neck, large head

▶ females are dull-colored but have distinctive white eye patch

▶ no other duck has the long, slicked-back crest

▶ rapid flight; they dodge easily between trees

# WOOD DUCK

*Aix sponsa*

rake Wood Ducks are considered by many to be the most beautiful of America's waterfowl. Hens, though less spectacular, are readily identified by white patches around the eye, and spotted breasts. Both sexes have tufts down the back of their necks and unusually long, square tails, that are especially obvious in flight. It is perhaps this feature that helps them to maneuver through trees and brake with surprising abruptness when landing on a branch. When flushed, they take off with whistling wings and a squealing, rising *oo-eek, oo-eek*. This apparently helps them to maintain contact with each other when flying through woods.

True to their name, these common ducks live along wooded shores and in forested bottomlands throughout their range. Though spotted occasionally in the far west and northern Rockies, their primary range extends from the Atlantic and Gulf coasts west to the Great Plains, and north into portions of Canada. In winter, they retreat to the southern states where waterways remain open. Unlike most flocking ducks, wood ducks only occasionally group up, usually in shallowly-flooded timber where there is a banquet of aquatic invertebrates, succulent greenery, roots, seeds, and acorns. Hens select foods rich in calcium and proteins, such as insects, in preparation for nesting.

Courting drakes swim near potential mates while tilting and turning about. This begins as early as late summer, and upon arriving on nesting grounds the following spring, most will have been paired off for months. Wood Ducks are one of a few waterfowl to nest in tree cavities, typically in holes left by broken branches or in large excavations created by woodpeckers. Laying commences in April or May and one white egg is laid each day. When the clutch of up to 15 eggs is complete, the hen begins incubation so they hatch fairly synchronously a month later.

Usually the morning after hatching, the hen begins clucking on the ground beneath the tree to entice her ducklings to jump from the nesting cavity. They may fall as far as 60 feet onto the hard ground without injury. When they are assembled, their mother sets off with them scrambling after her to find the nearest water. This journey, which may be as far as several hundred yards, is the most hazardous phase of their lives. Once in water, the tiny ducklings may still fall prey to bullfrogs, snapping turtles, and herons. Their mother may attempt to lure predators away from them with a broken wing act. Wood Ducks nest only once a year, and will use nest boxes.

## IDENTIFICATION TIPS

▶ male is easily recognized by the glossy green head and
white neck ring; body is grayish with a rusty chest

▶ female is mottled brown with a whitish tail

▶ both sexes have a violet-blue speculum that is bordered on both sides with white; in flight, these white
bars and the blue speculum are visible

♂

♀

# MALLARD
*Anas platyrhynchos*

allards are the best-known and possibly the most abundant ducks in the world. Mallards from Europe are the ancestors of almost all domestic ducks. Domestic Mallards sometimes revert to the wild and even cross with wild Mallards. Wild Mallards, however, can usually be recognized by their skittish behavior and tendency to form large flocks in fall and winter. They range nearly throughout North America. Drakes are sometimes called "green heads," especially by hunters. Hens are plain brown. Both sexes have a patch of blue-green secondary wing feathers, called a speculum, that shows in flight. They are about two feet in length when the neck is out-stretched, and they weigh two-and-a-half pounds. The Mallard's voice is the familiar, nasal quack.

Mallards are members of a group called dabbling ducks (also known as marsh ducks) — ducks that feed in shallow water by tipping in to take plants, seeds, and invertebrates from the bottom. Dabbling ducks are able to take off vertically, while other ducks must run across the water before becoming airborne. Mallards nest near ponds and lakes throughout much of the northeastern United States and across the continent to Alaska. Forced to the south when water freezes over, they migrate through the eastern states from October until December. They pass through as early as March on their return trip north. It is a delight to watch springtime Mallards in marshes because they are in their brightest breeding plumage and are fully involved in their highly-stylized courtship rituals. Often, two or more drakes will be seen flying in pursuit of a female.

Once mating occurs, females are left to the incubation and rearing chores. During that time, both sexes go through a mid- to late-summer molt that renders them flightless for a few weeks. A hen may lay as many as a dozen buff-colored eggs in a nest lined with her own down. Though most nests are at the water's edge, some may be surprisingly distant from water. Hens sometimes select unnatural nest sites such as planters, stone walls, and window wells. Eggs require about 28 days of incubation. The young are precocial, ready to follow their mothers within a few hours of hatching.

A close relative of the Mallard, the American Black Duck (*Anas rubripes*) nests in the northeastern United States and adjacent Canada, and winters as far north as Maine. The Black Duck sexes are identical, both resembling the dark female Mallard.

**IDENTIFICATION TIPS**

▶ both sexes have a pale blue area on the front edge of the wings

▶ male has a distinctive white facial crescent

▶ female is brown, mottled; late in the year, males may resemble females

▶ in flight, teal are recognized by their small size and tight flocks

▶ in flight, male Blue-wings show dark bellies, while Green-winged Teal show white bellies

▶ female Blue-wings are larger and longer billed than female Green-wings

♂

♀

# BLUE-WINGED TEAL

*Anas discors*

hese small ducks are more likely seen than others because their migration through the East takes place during the warmer parts of the spring and fall when people are more often enjoying the outdoors. Their name derives from the powder-blue patch on their wings, which is seen best in flight. Drakes have a diagnostic "half moon" on the face. Hens, because they alone provide parental care, are true to the duck pattern of being cryptically-colored so that they are less detectable when on the nest. Blue-wings are 15 inches long with neck outstretched and weigh about a pound. They are swift fliers, often forming compact flocks that course back and forth over a marsh before finally determining that they are clear for a landing. As dabbling ducks, they favor shallow marshes where they swim about and tip in to reach seeds, tender shoots, aquatic insects, and tiny crustaceans. When disturbed, they spring directly into flight with a flutter while emitting peeping sounds.

Though most known as spring and fall migrants, Blue wings breed in association with wetlands in the northern counties of New York and a few areas in northern New England. Their breeding range extends westward across the continent, regions that supply the majority of the fall migrants that are seen along the Atlantic Coast in fall. Compared to other ducks, Blue-wings are unusually early fall migrants, most moving through during September. This early migration occurs because, unlike most ducks, many Blue-wings travel all the way to Peru, Brazil, and Argentina to winter. Upon their return in March and April, most Blue-wings have paired off. Nests are constructed on dry ground near water and concealed from above by arching vegetation. Ten to 13 cream-colored eggs constitute a clutch. The hen incubates them until they hatch in 23 to 24 days and then leads her precocial ducklings to water.

Blue-winged Teal are slightly larger than their cousins, Green-winged Teal (*Anas crecca*), which lack the blue shoulder and are much later migrants in Fall.

## IDENTIFICATION TIPS

▶ their long wings are held in an arched position; the crook is marked with black which confirms identification
▶ the head is mainly white, suggesting a Bald Eagle, but it has a broad black cheek patch
▶ in flight, they flap more than they sail; wingbeats are slow and deep
▶ call is a series of loud, clear whistles
▶ North America's only raptor that plunges into the water to catch fish

# OSPREY

*Pandion haliaetus*

spreys are conspicuous both physically and behaviorally. In the East, most Ospreys nest along the coast and along major rivers, estuaries, and bays, such as the Chesapeake. They are also prevalent on streams and lakes of upper New York State and New England. When in the air, they are usually noticed because of their long wings, which span five feet and arch like a gull's with a dark patch at the bend. The body of the bird is about 2 feet long. Though primarily white below, their wings and tail are barred with brown. Ospreys are dark brown above. They have dark masks across their yellow eyes.

Also called "fish hawks," Ospreys search coastal waters, lakes, and streams by alternately gliding and flapping. Upon sighting a fish near the surface, they may hover briefly before diving from as high as 100 feet to plunge into the water feet first. Once a fish is securely grasped by the feet, an Osprey carries it from the water, repositioning it so that the head is forward and thus more aerodynamic. Ospreys will typically wiggle in flight to shake water from their feathers.

Like other members of the raptor family, Ospreys build large, stick nests usually in the crowns of tall trees. Ospreys sometimes use unnatural structures for their nests, such as buoys, channel markers, utility poles, and even Ferris wheels. Wildlife managers have helped populations by erecting artificial nesting platforms. Ospreys lay two to four heavily splotched white eggs which are incubated for 30 to 35 days entirely by the female. Her mate delivers food while she is on the nest and helps her to feed the rapidly growing nestlings. A brood of three requires six pounds of fish daily. Young Ospreys fly from the nest when two to three months of age.

Ospreys are one of few species to range around the world. The majority of North American Ospreys winter in South America. Although they can be found in any state during their spring and fall migration, their breeding range extends across the northern states and southern Canada, and along both coasts. One satellite-tracked individual that left St. Paul, Minnesota, in September was found at weekly intervals in Missouri, Texas, Mexico, Costa Rica, Venezuela, Peru and, finally, Bolivia, where it made its winter home.

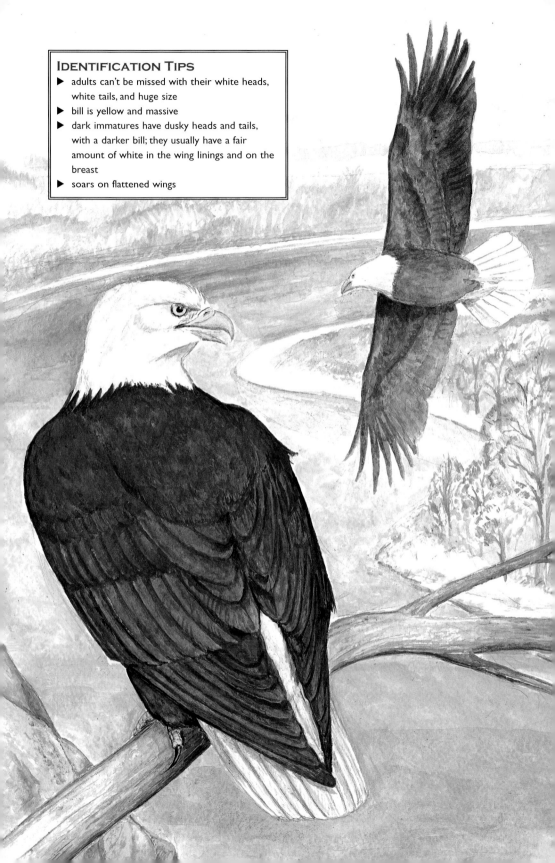

## IDENTIFICATION TIPS

▶ adults can't be missed with their white heads, white tails, and huge size

▶ bill is yellow and massive

▶ dark immatures have dusky heads and tails, with a darker bill; they usually have a fair amount of white in the wing linings and on the breast

▶ soars on flattened wings

# BALD EAGLE

*Haliaeetus leucocephalus*

ur National Bird is known to all despite being only occasionally sighted in the wild. The Bald Eagle is a migratory species that nests in proximity to lakes and streams during the summer months in the northern part of the eastern states. During the coldest part of the winter they migrate to the southern part of their breeding range and all the way to the Gulf and Atlantic coasts. They are most likely to be seen along major rivers and the unfrozen parts of bays, such as the Chesapeake.

Typically, Bald Eagles perch high in shoreline trees to keep a lookout for prey and to avoid disturbance. In this prominent location, their diagnostic white head and tail are eye-catching, contrasting vividly with their dark brown body. At nearly three feet in length and weighing up to 15 pounds, their size is difficult to judge until they are in the air. It is then that their deep, plodding wing-beats attest to their size. When they set their wings to soar, they exhibit an airplane-like profile that spans seven feet.

As a white-headed adult, the Bald Eagle is one of the easiest birds to identify. Individuals younger than five years, however, lack the white head and tail and vary from being solid dark brown to being blotched throughout with white. These juveniles, which are otherwise similar to adults in size, habitat, and behavior, compose about one-third of the eagle population. Wintering flocks typically contain both age groups.

Fish compose most of the Bald Eagle's diet. When a fish is sighted, the predator will swoop low over the water to dip its powerful, sharp-taloned feet beneath the surface to snag prey. Opportunists, they also scavenge for dead fish on shores and the dead and dying ducks and geese that result from large concentrations of migrating waterfowl. Bald Eagles will also scavenge road-side kills.

Bald Eagles build the largest nest of any bird. Composed of sticks, nests typically exceed three feet across and two feet in depth. Nests are situated on strong branches near the tops of huge trees, and are perennial, meaning that the eagles will return to the same nest each year and continue to build and reconstruct it. Some eagles have been known to use the same nest for over 35 years. Two to three white eggs are laid in March, hatch in April, and the young fledge in June. Since the banning of DDT in 1972, Bald Eagles are becoming more common.

## SHARP-SHINNED HAWK

- ▶ small, slim hawk with short, rounded wings and long tail
- ▶ flies with several quick beats and a glide
- ▶ Cooper's Hawk is obviously larger with a rounded tail; Sharp-shin tail is narrower and more square-cut
- ▶ male Cooper's and female Sharp-shin resemble each other closely making identification difficult

## AMERICAN TREE SPARROW

- ▶ the large central breast spot and a solid red-brown cap distinguish these sparrows from others
- ▶ bill is dark above, yellow below
- ▶ two white wingbars
- ▶ seen in large flocks in winter

# SHARP-SHINNED HAWK
*Accipiter striatus*

# AMERICAN TREE SPARROW
*Spizella arborea*

Sharp-shinned Hawks are small, slim woodland hawks that are adapted to prey on other birds. They have fairly short, rounded wings, and long tails. These features enable bursts of speed and maneuverability when pursuing small birds among branches. When perched, the tail extends several inches beyond the tip of the folded wings. Sharp-shinned Hawks average 11 inches in length with females being about one-third larger than males. As adults, their upper parts are blue-gray and their breasts, bellies, and shanks are barred with flecks of orangish-brown. Their tails are boldly barred and their eyes red. Juveniles, which seem nearly as common as adults, have brown backs flecked with white, and streaks of brown on their otherwise light breasts. Juveniles have finely barred tails and yellow eyes. Both age groups have bright yellow legs.

These reclusive hawks are perhaps best known because of their habit of frequenting neighborhoods where bird feeders concentrate small birds, thus making predation easy. They are difficult to pick out among the branches until the moment of the ambush. Captured prey is taken to a favorite perch, called a "butcher block," where the predator, while furtively glancing about for thieves, quickly de-feathers and consumes it.

Sharp-shinned Hawks and their look-alike larger relative, the Cooper's Hawk (*Accipiter cooperii*), are most noticed during winter. Many, however, summer and nest in forests of the northeast. An even larger relative, the Northern Goshawk (*Accipiter gentilis*) nests in northern New York State and New England, and winters throughout the East.

Sharp-shinned Hawks build stick nests, usually well-concealed in evergreens. The males do nearly all of the hunting during incubation and into the nestling stage. Four to five white eggs (often marked with brown) typically hatch in June, and the young depart the nest a month later.

American Tree Sparrows are winter visitors from the far north. They are five-and-a-half inches in length and identified by their rusty cap, white wingbars, and the dark central spot on their plain gray breast. Flocks of them inhabit weedy fields and brushy wastelands during their winter stay.

American Tree Sparrow    Sharp-shinned Hawk

# BROAD-WINGED HAWK
*Buteo platypterus*

These woodland birds of prey are buteos, hawks that soar on broad wings with tails fanned. At only 13 to 15 inches in length and with a wingspan of 32 to 36 inches, they are North America's smallest buteo. As adults, their breasts are cross-hatched with rust and their tails have broad black bands. The tails of those younger than two years have numerous narrow bands. In flight, soaring Broad-winged Hawks exhibit white underwings with dark edging. They emit a high, thin whistle, occasionally while in flight but often from the woods' interior. This is sometimes dismissed as the call of the Eastern Wood-Pewee.

Broad-winged Hawks typically hunt from a perch, taking small mammals and birds, insects, reptiles, and amphibians. They nest through most of the eastern half of the United States, primarily deep within broad-leaf and coniferous forests. Nesting is initiated in late April and May. Stick platforms one to two feet across are constructed high in the crotches of trees. Females lay two to four white eggs that are incubated by her alone for 28 to 31 days. The young depart the nest at one month of age. Broad-winged Hawks nest only once each year.

Because of their secretive habits when nesting, Broad-winged Hawks are not easily seen. The best opportunity to view them is during their impressive migrations. Sometimes hundreds can be seen overhead at one time, circling together on rising columns of air and then gliding down to catch another thermal to carry them upward. These impressive displays are most likely seen during September and shortly after the birds have departed their night roosts, between nine and eleven in the morning. The best days to witness the migrations are bright, warm days, especially when there is a breeze out of the north. Broad-winged Hawks seem to follow north to south oriented mountain ranges, such as the Appalachians. They winter on islands in the Caribbean and in Central and South America.

# RED-TAILED HAWK
*Buteo jamaicensis*

Red-tailed Hawks are by far the most commonly seen bird of prey in North America. These are large, open-country hawks. No matter the season, it is possible to hear their thin, raspy screams and see one or two circling overhead with broad wings set and tail fanned. From below, the tail appears solidly tan unless the sun shines through it or the bird tips, revealing its reddish upper side. With wings spanning four feet and a length approaching two feet, Red-tailed Hawks are impressive whether soaring or perched.

When these familiar birds of prey are perched, it is usually their gleaming white breasts that catch the eye first. Most have a band of dark flecks across the belly. There is great color variation among individuals however. Some are nearly solid brown, except for the tail, and some are nearly white. Even tail color is not a conclusive identifier because those younger than two years of age have finely barred tails on a brown or rusty background.

Red-tailed Hawks prey primarily on mice, rabbits, ground squirrels, and snakes. They are most conspicuous in winter because individuals from the northern breeding range have migrated south and add to the more southern, year-round population. They pair up in late winter and by late February or March, each pair begins construction of a nest, typically in the high crotch of a large tree along a woodland edge. Their stick nests, two to three feet across and up to two feet deep, are easy to see before leaf-out. Two to three chicken-egg-sized, speckled brown eggs are laid in March. The month-long incubation is performed entirely by the female while her mate feeds her on the nest. The heads of the downy young may be first seen above the nest rim in April, and they fledge during late May and June.

**IDENTIFICATION TIPS**

▶ about the size of a jay
▶ no other small hawk has a
   rusty back or tail
▶ frequently hovers for prey on
   rapidly beating wings
▶ in comparison, Sharp-shinned
   Hawk has rounded wings and
   gray or brown back and tail

# AMERICAN KESTREL

*Falco sparverius*

merica's smallest falcons are easily seen because they tend to perch on power lines along roadways. They are recognized by their blunt-headed, neckless profile and rather long tails. In flight, they exhibit the relatively long, pointed wings characteristic of falcons. Males, which among falcons are the smallest of the two sexes, are nine inches in length and gaudily-colored with blue wings and orangish backs and tails. Females are nearly a foot in length and lack the blue on the wings and the brilliant russet coloration. Both sexes have a vertical black bar on the side of the head and a black "whisker" extending down from the bill. Like other raptors, they have sharp talons for holding the prey and a hooked bill for tearing it apart.

American Kestrels reside in grasslands where the vegetation is tall enough to accommodate mice and voles, their most common prey, but short enough so that the birds can see the rodents moving about. They drop swiftly onto prey from a perch or from a hovering point in the sky. They also eat large insects, snakes, lizards, and frogs. They rarely employ their falcon speed to take small birds. Their alternate name, "Sparrowhawk," is more fitting for the Sharp-shinned Hawk.

American Kestrels nest throughout the region and northward to the tree line in Canada. They winter where snow cover is of short duration, being generally absent from northern New York State and New England. Where they do winter, they gravitate to roadsides and can be quite conspicuous. Also, migrants from the north join those that reside at the lower latitudes year round.

Beginning in April, flying pairs emit *killy killy killy* cries as they pair off for the upcoming nesting season. While migrants depart for the north, residents move to areas in the vicinity where there are cavities for nesting. In addition to holes in trees, they select niches in walls and specially-designed kestrel boxes. They use little to no nesting material. The female lays four to five brown, speckled eggs. They hatch in a month and the young fledge a month later. Pairs will sometimes raise a second brood later in the summer.

# RUFFED GROUSE

*Bonasa umbellus*

These plump, 15-inch-long grouse are game birds in some states. They are most often encountered by people who live in or visit birch- or aspen-dominated forests in New England, New York, Pennsylvania, West Virginia, and the mountainous regions of Virginia and Maryland. Their range extends west through North America's northern forests. Through much of the year, Ruffed Grouse go unnoticed. But from April through May, males attract attention with their unique courtship ritual, a behavior called "drumming." At that season, they perch on logs, often a hollow one selected for its resonating qualities. They beat their wings against their sides to produce a very low drumming sound that carries for hundreds of yards through the forest. Each "drum roll" begins slowly and increases to a blurring rapidity over a period of several seconds. Drumming is most intense just before sunrise, and can occur sporadically throughout the year.

The grouse's consumption of buds, catkins, and succulent shoots helps to explain their association with young forests where these foods are available near the ground. When winter snows are deep, however, they become arboreal to obtain buds high in the canopies of aspen trees. After the reproductively receptive females have successfully responded to "drumming" males, they construct nests on the ground, often at the base of a tree. She lays one buff-colored egg every day or two, for a period of two to three weeks. When her clutch of 10 to 14 eggs is complete, she initiates incubation so that they hatch synchronously in 21 to 24 days. The chicks follow their mother and feed almost immediately after hatching. At three months of age, they are on their own.

**IDENTIFICATION TIPS**
▶ rather noisy, repetitive call
▶ 2 black upper breast bands; chick has 1 band
▶ in flight, displays orange on the upper tail and lower back, longish tail, white wing stripe
▶ tail is longer than other plovers

# KILLDEER

*Charadrius vociferus*

he *kill-dee-kill-dee-kill-dee* cries of these common plovers can be heard between their arrival in March until their departure in October. Essentially white below and brown above, they are distinguished by two black bands across the upper chest. They run about rapidly on spindly legs, often stopping abruptly with a slight bow. Or they skip into flight and course low over the ground for a short distance before landing with a run. Their rusty rump can be seen when they are in low level flight. When overhead, the Killdeer's white undersides and long, pointed wings are reminiscent of a gull's.

These conspicuous birds frequent short-grass, gravelly, or barren areas such as closely-cropped pastures, driveways, and open construction sites. Though members of the shorebird family, they do not require a shoreline, although sometimes they are sighted on beaches and river gravel bars. Their primary foods, insects and worms, are more available where the earth is moist.

Killdeers build no nest but simply create a shallow depression for their eggs in a pebble substrate. Like many ground-nesting birds, Killdeers feign injury to lure predators from their nests and young. It is not unusual to hear their plaintive trill and see them floundering about on the ground when they believe their nest is threatened. This strategy is successful because the splotchy brown pattern of the eggs matches the gray, tan, or brown gravel on which they are laid. There are usually four eggs with pointy ends that project inward to fit neatly together in a clutch. They hatch in 24 to 26 days.

The young are precocial and follow their parents soon after hatching, seeming little more than puff-balls on toothpicks. They freeze instinctively when danger arises. In a few weeks, they are on their own and the parent birds can nest a second time. Killdeers breed throughout most of North America and winter in the southern states and Mexico.

Lesser Yellowlegs

Spotted Sandpiper

# SPOTTED SANDPIPER
*Actitis macularia*

Of the 30-plus members of the sandpiper family in North America, this is the only species that nests throughout most of the United States. Most other sandpipers are migrants to and from Arctic nesting grounds. Because they nest here, Spotted Sandpipers are often seen in summer along lakes and rivers. These seven-inch shorebirds are recognized by their spotted breast, light eye-line, and their habit of tilting back and forth on spindly legs as they search shorelines for aquatic invertebrates such as midges and mayflies. The bill is orange but darkly tipped, and the legs are yellow. When approached too closely, Spotted Sandpipers fly low on quivering wings to land farther down the shore, while showing the diagnostic light line in each wing, and white, finely-barred outer tail feathers. The sexes are identical in appearance. Seldom is more than one bird seen at a time.

Spotted Sandpipers are one of relatively few bird species in which the sex roles, regarding parental care, are often reversed. Females arrive on breeding grounds a few days before males, in April and May, presumably to establish nesting territories. After the female lays her typical clutch of four buff-colored eggs in June, the male does most of the incubation during the three weeks until they hatch. His mate may assist him at first; then she seems to lose interest and the male is left to tend the growing chicks until they are on their own. During this time, the female may mate with one or more additional males, involving them in parental responsibilities as well.

Spotted Sandpipers migrate in late summer and can appear at coastal shores while on their way to the Gulf Coast and Central America. From fall through early spring, their breasts are plain rather than spotted, but they can still be identified by the light line in the open wing and the constant bobbing as they walk about.

The three birds shown flying in the background are Lesser Yellowlegs (*Tringa flavipes*). These slender, longer-legged sandpipers are occasionally sighted in the same wetlands as Spotted Sandpipers.

# RING-BILLED GULL
*Larus delawarensis*

These medium-sized, common gulls nest in Canada and the bordering edge of the United States, and spend their winters along the Atlantic Coast and across the southern states. In between, they can be seen along almost any stream or lake. They are 16 inches long and have a wingspan of four feet. The name stems from the black ring around the tip of adults' yellow bills. Mature birds have white bodies, gray upper-parts, black wingtips, and yellow feet. Those younger than two years are mottled brown, have a black tip on a pinkish bill, and pink legs.

Many people think of gulls as "seagulls," and are surprised to learn of those associated with fresh water, such as Ring-billed Gulls. Ring-billed Gulls breed in colonies near northern lakes and rivers in areas with sparse vegetation. Each pair raises an average of two young each year. Ring-bills move south in late fall as waterways freeze over. Some remain in the north where spillways, power plants, and rapids keep water open. They eat small fish that come near the surface, and hundreds of individuals might be seen flying about or resting on the ice or water at especially favorable feeding areas. Opportunistic feeders, they also eat insects, earthworms, and human handouts. They often visit garbage dumps.

Another freshwater-associated gull in the East is the smaller Bonaparte's Gull (*Larus philadelphia*). Bonaparte's Gulls also migrate from Canada to winter in coastal waters. Though adults are gray and white with black wingtips, as are Ring-billed Gulls, their wingspan is less than three feet, they have pink legs, a black bill, and a black ear-spot in winter. A similarly-sized gull with a black head, the Laughing Gull (*Larus atricilla*), summers and nests along the Atlantic Coast.

**IDENTIFICATION TIPS**

▶ adults are distinguished from the Ring-billed Gull by the Herring Gull's heavier build, larger size, and pink legs

▶ heavy yellow bill with a red spot

▶ first and second-year Herrings are much darker tailed than Ring-billed

# HERRING GULL

*Larus argentatus*

The Herring Gull is the largest familiar gull in the East. As adults, they exhibit the usual gull pattern of gray and white with black wingtips, but they are 20 inches long and have a wingspan of four-and-a-half feet. Their legs are pink and the bill yellow. First-year birds are entirely brown; those in their second year are becoming gray and white, but still have brown wings and tails. Herring Gulls are often seen perched on prominences or soaring on long, narrow wings. Their most common calls are loud *keows* and *yelps*.

Herring Gulls winter along the Atlantic Coast and breed along it to as far south as North Carolina. Otherwise, their breeding range extends through New England and upstate New York through the upper Great Lakes across Canada. They also range through most of the Northern Hemisphere and are one of the most abundant gulls in the world.

Herring Gulls are opportunistic feeders. Inland, they primarily take small fish; crabs, clams, and sea urchins constitute much of the diet of those that feed in intertidal zones. Herring Gulls also steal prey from other birds and scavenge behind garbage scows and in dumps. At sea, they feed around fishing boats and foraging whales.

Herring Gulls nest colonially, usually on rocky ledges near water. They return to nesting areas in March and build grass cups to hold their clutch of two to three olive-speckled eggs. Both sexes incubate the eggs and feed the young. Incubation requires 24 to 28 days. Young chicks peck at a red dot near the tip of the parent's bill, provoking the regurgitation of food. The chicks continue to be fed by both parents for up to 15 weeks, long after they are fully-grown and capable of flight.

## IDENTIFICATION TIPS

▶ typical birds are gray with a whitish rump, two
black wing bars, and a broad dark tail band;
many color variations though

# ROCK DOVE
*Columba livia*

igeons, as they are usually called, are familiar to all. Perhaps because they eat agricultural grains, they have lived in association with humans since the early days of civilization. Native to the Old World, some individuals first became domesticated over 3,000 years ago. Through selective breeding, they were developed into breeds specialized for food, visual appeal, and message delivery as in the example of homing pigeons. As the world has been explored and settled, pigeons have been transported widely and have become feral nearly everywhere.

Caged pigeons were listed among the supplies brought to the Jamestown Colony in 1610, so they were introduced to the New World very early. They now range across North America with the exception of the far north. The various colors in current wild populations attest to their human-modified ancestry. The original wild type — birds with charcoal bodies, light-gray wings, and two black wing bars — still predominates in the population.

Maintaining their close association with people, pigeon flocks are prevalent in cities, towns, and on farms. Superb fliers, they course through the sky at over 60 miles per hour. Common flight displays include clapping the wing-tips over the back and gliding with wings held in a V. To impress females, males strut about, puff their crops, fan their tails, stretch, bow and rotate in place, while emitting a rolling *coo*.

Courtship and nesting can occur during all but the coldest weeks of the year. Nesting colonies are usually in man-made structures including niches on buildings, under bridges, and in barns. Their two white eggs require 20 days of incubation. Squabs are fed a regurgitated "pigeon milk" by both parents during the month that they are growing in the nest. Soon after fledging their young, or sometimes before, the pair begins nesting again.

# MOURNING DOVE

*Zenaida macroura*

he East's native dove lives in a broad array of habitats from suburban yards to rural fields. They also range throughout the lower 48 states. They measure 10 to 12 inches in length, have a buff-gray plumage, a relatively small head, and pointed tail. Comparatively numerous, they are readily seen along roadways as they perch on power lines or pick up bits of sand to aid digestion of grains and seeds. Startled birds burst into flight, flaring the white outer feathers of their tails as their wings whistle. The whistling is also heard as they brake for a landing. Their soft, four- to five-parted *coo*, given from a perch, seems distant and melancholy, giving this dove its name.

After returning from the southern states in February and March, Mourning Doves prepare for mating by cooing, mutual preening, and billing — a behavior involving the interlocking of bills. Males embark on courtship flights in which they clap their wingtips together during exaggerated flaps as they gain altitude. Then they set their wings and glide downward through a long course that takes them back to the female and their chosen nest site.

Nests are typically built in the forks of horizontal branches. Pines seem preferred. The female constructs the nest by fitting sticks around herself that the male delivers by landing directly on her back. Two eggs are standard. They are white and sometimes visible from beneath through thin nests. Parents take turns sitting on the eggs. It takes two weeks for the eggs to hatch and another two weeks for the young to fly. As with Rock Doves, Mourning Dove nestlings are fed "pigeon milk." Pairs will nest two to four times during a season.

Pairs may be seen flying together well beyond the nesting season due to their strong, enduring bonds. Doves form flocks in fall and migration commences in the northern states in September. Some doves linger as far north as New York State and along the coast to as far north as Maine. Wintering doves sometimes visit bird feeding stations, favoring cracked corn that is scattered on the ground.

# BLACK-BILLED CUCKOO

*Coccyzus erythropthalmus*

lthough most people have heard of cuckoos (perhaps via cuckoo clocks), few know them by sight. Yet cuckoos are one of our most common birds, at least through the eastern half of the United States. The cuckoo species that ranges through most of the East is the Black-billed Cuckoo. These are slender, 11-inch birds that are deep brown above and white below. Their bill, of course, is black; their long tail is lightly barred beneath. A thin border of red skin encircles each eye. Their call, which is often the only evidence that they are around, is a rapid series of three to four *coos*. Though it sounds distant, people who take the time to look may find the originator nearby.

Black-billed Cuckoos are most numerous north of the New York City latitude. They also range southward at cooler elevations. Their southern counterpart, the Yellow-billed Cuckoo (*Coccyzus americanus*), mainly takes up residence to the south of New York State and is common in the lower elevations of Virginia and Maryland. They are also brown above, white below, and the same shape and size. However, they have contrasting black and white bars on the under-tail, rust on the outer wing feathers, and a yellow bill. Their lazy, eight to ten note call begins with a *ka-ka-ka* and ends in a hollow-sounding *kowlp-kowlp-kowlp*.

Cuckoos typically arrive on breeding grounds in May. Their flight is slow, low, and direct, frequently resulting in collisions with cars and house windows. They are one of few birds that eat hairy and spiny caterpillars. In fact, they eat them so regularly that the inner surfaces of their stomachs are furry as a result of the many spines that have pierced the lining. Cuckoos build flimsy, stick nests, usually in trees. They typically raise two broods each summer, laying three to four blue-green eggs per clutch. When food is most abundant, such as during webworm outbreaks, cuckoos will lay up to three sets of five eggs in a season.

Because of the rapid development of their young — only 11 days of incubation and an additional nine days to fledging — cuckoos seem adapted to be brood parasites, as are Brown-headed Cowbirds and the Old World cuckoos. American cuckoos, however, rarely lay their eggs in the nests of other birds.

**IDENTIFICATION TIPS**
- ▶ no other eared owl is bright red-brown
- ▶ young birds may lack conspicuous ears
- ▶ all other eastern "eared" owls are obviously larger

# EASTERN SCREECH-OWL

*Otus asio*

These small, seven to nine inch tall owls resemble miniature Great Horned Owls because of their "ear" tufts. They are most numerous in the south, fading out to the northeast of the New York-Vermont border. They occur in two color phases — rusty and gray — that persist despite the fact that they share the same range. There is regional variation in the predominance of the two phases however. Most individuals east of the Appalachians are rufous, while most to the west and north are gray. When rusty and gray owls mate, their individual offspring are either one phase or the other, not a blend of the two. As with most nocturnal creatures, it is their sound that reveals their presence. Their most common vocalization is a long, descending *whinny*. They also deliver an even-toned trill and, when agitated, the piercing scream that has given them their name.

These small nonmigratory owls are extremely nocturnal, preying on animals that become active after dark, such as mice. They also capture small birds from night roosts. Insects, crayfish, and earthworms constitute much of their diet during the warmer months of the year. They favor fragmented forests including woodlots and forested suburbs. They are distributed as far west as the Rocky Mountains. In New England and northern New York State, they are out-numbered by an even smaller, "earless" owl, the Northern Saw-whet Owl (*Aegolius acadicus*).

Eastern Screech-Owls nest in tree hollows and in lofts and niches of farm buildings, a behavior that regularly puts them in competition with squirrels and European Starlings. Egg-laying occurs from March to June, with a clutch containing as many as six white eggs. The male feeds the incubating female during the latter days of the month-long incubation period. Because incubation begins with the first egg laid, the eggs hatch over sequential days and the young are noticeably different in size. They typically depart the nesting cavity in the order that they were hatched at about one month of age.

**AMERICAN CROW**
- ▶ large, completely black bird, glossed with purple cast in strong sunlight
- ▶ Common Raven is larger; has a wedge-shaped tail

**GREAT HORNED OWL**
- ▶ large, with ear tufts or "horns"
- ▶ heavily barred beneath
- ▶ has a conspicuous white throat bib
- ▶ twice the size of the crows that often harass it

# GREAT HORNED OWL
*Bubo virginianus*

# AMERICAN CROW
*Corvus brachyrhynchos*

reat Horned Owls are large, powerful predators of the night that are common in the East and across North America. They are one-and-a-half feet long, have wingspans exceeding four feet, and can weigh up to five pounds. Swooping down with clawed feet forward, they strike with such force that they can instantly kill prey larger than themselves. Great Horned Owls often smell of the skunks they have attacked, attesting to their fearlessness. They are identified by their "ear" tufts, white bibs, and huge yellow eyes. Their muffled *who-hoo-hoo-hooo* can be heard the year around, but especially during wintertime courtship. Great Horned Owls do not build nests. Instead, they use prior nests of large birds such as hawks and herons, or lay eggs in such places as barn lofts. Their eggs are white, nearly spherical, and typically number two or three per clutch. Nesting commences the earliest of any of our native birds, in January and February, so that nestlings are growing and fledge in April and May in synchrony with the emergence of the spring's first crop of young field mice and rabbits.

At 17 inches in length and with a wingspan of three feet, American Crows are the East's largest "songbird," except for the Common Raven (*Corvus corax*). They are numerous throughout the country and in a variety of habitats. They eat a variety of plant and animal material, and can even become predacious when the opportunity arises. Though typically noisy, crows can become mysteriously secretive around nests, which are usually hidden in pines or other concealing trees. Construction of stick nests commences in March. Four to five greenish-blue, speckled eggs hatch in 18 days, and the young fledge at around 35 days of age. Crows are migratory, but wintering flocks are found as far north as Canada. Increasingly, they are becoming common in urban areas. Renowned for their intelligence, crows are highly social. They often gang up on birds that they consider threats such as hawks, eagles, and especially, owls. At a disadvantage during the day, Great Horned Owls are often driven about amid the angry cawing of mobbing crows. Rarely, an owl will reach out with its foot and nab a crow that approaches too closely.

Great Horned Owl    American Crow

**IDENTIFICATION TIPS**

► large; gray-brown; puffy-headed
► large, moist brown eyes
► chest is barred; belly is streaked lengthwise
► white spots on back
► other owls, except Barn Owl, have yellow eyes

# BARRED OWL

*Strix varia*

ike other nocturnal birds, Barred Owls are best detected by sound. Fortunately for birders, Barred Owls deliver one of the most recognizable of calls. It is a series of hoots with a distinctive rhythm, often rendered as *who cooks for you . . . who cooks for you all*. The "all" ("aw") at the end of the call is characteristic. Barred Owls may be heard during any night of year and occasionally during daylight as well. Both males and females hoot and, when in full concert, will emit wild *yawls* and *chuckles*. Although one of our larger owls, Barred owls are not quite as large as Great Horned Owls. They average 17 inches in length and have wingspans of about 44 inches. Unlike Great Horneds, Barred Owls have no "ear" tufts, resulting in a rounded head. Additionally, they have dark rather than yellow eyes, and their plumage is barred.

Barred Owls are permanent residents from the East Coast through the mid-United States. There is a disjunct population in the Pacific Northwest. This owl is most associated with forested bottomlands and swamps, especially where there are large unbroken forests containing mature and decaying trees. Substantial populations occur in the Appalachians north through the Adirondacks. The Barred Owl's feet are small as compared to a Great Horned Owl's, being more suited to small prey such as voles, mice, and shrews. Because of their proximity to rivers, they also eat frogs, snakes, and crayfish.

Female Barred Owls lay two to three roundish, white eggs directly on the bottom of a hollow in a large broken or decaying tree. A pair may use the same nest site for many years in succession. The eggs hatch in 28 to 33 days. As is typical of owls, young leave the nest at a few weeks of age, well before they can fly. These flightless owlets are called "branchers" and, as they grow and test their wings, they will ultimately flutter to the ground. Well-meaning people sometimes pick them up, believing them to be abandoned. In reality, their parents will find and feed them nightly for several more weeks, often until they are beyond four months of age, when they are able to hunt on their own.

IDENTIFICATION TIPS
▶ slim-winged; gray-brown; often seen high in the air
▶ flies with easy strokes, changing quickly to quicker erratic strokes
▶ broad white bar across the long, pointed wings
▶ male has a white bar across its notched tail and a white throat

# COMMON NIGHTHAWK

*Chordeiles minor*

ommon Nighthawks are nine inches long with two foot wingspans, and are often seen over towns near dusk. When illuminated by city lights from below, a white bar can be seen on each of their long, swept-back, pointed wings. Where one nighthawk is seen, there most certainly will be others, swooping low then climbing skyward again while repeatedly emitting *peent* calls.

They are also called "bullbats," and this fanciful name is little more misleading than "nighthawk," as they are seldom active after dark and are not hawks at all. Instead, they are members of a group known as *goatsuckers*, a name that also has a peculiar origin. An ancient myth, promulgated by Aristotle, maintained that a European relative of the Common Nighthawk used its wide mouth to suck milk from goats. In reality, the unusually broad mouths of the birds of this group are used to capture large flying insects, such as june bugs, cicadas, and moths.

These aerial insectivores become conspicuous over our cities with the return of warm, humid weather in early May. Not only are they benefited by the street lights that concentrate their prey, but the flat gravel roofs of downtown buildings offer a nesting alternative to the gravelly, barren areas that they used historically. Males court females by repeatedly diving from as high as 80 feet before flaring their wings and tail to produce a loud, low *boom*, usually over a prospective nest site. Perceived threats, such as humans who approach nests too closely, are sometimes startled by these diving birds. A person who has had a Common Nighthawk *boom* near his head, will long remember the event.

Common Nighthawks nest only once each season, usually beginning in May. Their two eggs are heavily speckled with brown. They hatch in 18 days. Rooftop nests can become dangerously hot for both eggs and young. Although fed by their parents, the young are able to move about somewhat to locate bits of shade during summer days and to escape other dangers. Chicks are able to fly at 18 days of age.

Common Nighthawks nest throughout most of North America. In August and September, hundreds can sometimes be seen migrating overhead during the daylight hours toward their winter home in South America.

# WHIP-POOR-WILL

*Caprimulgus vociferus*

he strange name of this nocturnal bird is a verbal rendition of its call. This three-syllable whistle emanates from wooded areas, beginning in April. Just as daytime birds are most vocal at dawn and dusk, Whip-poor-wills sing most at the onset and conclusion of their period of activity, during the twilight minutes before dawn and after sunset. They often whistle all night, especially during a full moon, delivering hundreds of *whip-poor-wills* in quick succession. When this happens near homes, they are sometimes threatened by disturbed sleepers; however, most people are quick to defend what they consider to be a symbol of the wilderness that surrounds them.

These nine-inch-long birds have broad mouths for catching moths, june bugs, and cicadas. Unlike their Common Nighthawk "cousins," Whip-poor-wills seldom fly where they can be seen. Night travelers of rural gravel roads may see them sitting like chunks of wood on the roadway, their eyes glowing red in the headlights. Occasionally they are noticed during the day, resting longitudinally on horizontal limbs, in an attempt to blend in as part of the branch.

Whip-poor-wills breed from the East Coast to the Great Plains. They are most numerous in the southeastern states and their abundance diminishes in the northeastern states. If they are flushed into flight from the forest floor during May and June, there is probably a nest nearby. Whip-poor-wills assemble no nesting material. They simply lay their two white, gray-mottled eggs directly on dry leaves. The eggs hatch in 19 days. Young are covered with silky down and are somewhat precocial, being able to shuffle about soon after hatching. A few weeks later, they are capable of their first flight. They nest only once a season. Calling subsides during mid-summer, when most young are being reared, but resumes briefly before their departure south in September. They winter along the Gulf Coast and through Central America.

# CHIMNEY SWIFT

*Chaetura pelagica*

espite their familiarity in towns and cities across eastern North America, Chimney Swifts remain one of our bird curiosities. These sooty-gray birds are invariably seen in flight, their cylindrical, five-inch bodies propelled rapidly on slender, stiff wings. It has been suggested that they resemble "flying cigars." People sometimes mistake them for bats. They often course this way and that in little squadrons of two or three, chattering noisily, just above rooftops.

Chimney Swifts spend more time aloft than any other land bird, consuming flying insects, drinking, bathing, courting, and even copulating while on the wing. They are seldom seen perched, as this occurs only within an enclosure, commonly a chimney. Here they cling by their otherwise little-used toes while propping themselves up vertically with stiff tails.

April marks the return of these long distance migrants. Nesting commences in May. Their nests are composed of small, dead twigs that they snap from the tips of branches while in flight. These are fastened together forming a half-saucer on the inside of the chimney with a glue formed by the bird's own saliva. It is this saliva, from a different swift, that is used to make "bird's nest soup" in the Orient. Several Chimney Swift nests may be built in a single chimney, depending on its size. Each nest holds three to six white eggs. They hatch in 18 to 21 days. Fledglings that are unable to fly well sometimes fall into fireplaces.

Chimney Swifts assemble into flocks of thousands between the completion of their nesting season, in August, and their departure, in October. At dusk, these birds swirl about their favorite chimneys in hordes, passing over the top again and again before fluttering in to roost for the night. Over 10,000 were once counted entering a single industrial stack in Pennsylvania. After years of uncertainty, the Chimney Swift wintering ground was located when a Peruvian Indian was discovered wearing a necklace strung with the tiny leg bands put on nestlings by researchers in North America.

**IDENTIFICATION TIPS**

▶ male has glowing, fiery-red throat; iridescent green back; forked tail

▶ female lacks red throat; has outer tail feathers tipped with white

# RUBY-THROATED HUMMINGBIRD
*Archilochus colubris*

he smallest of the eastern North America's birds is a mere three inches in length and weighs little more than a penny. Males have throats that gleam crimson in certain angles of light. Females have white throats with fine, dark speckles and white corners on their tails. Juveniles are colored like females except that the throats of those approaching a year of age are speckled with red.

These amazingly tiny, warm-blooded creatures require considerable amounts of high-energy foods to support their rapid metabolism. Hummingbirds fulfill this requirement with the carbohydrate-rich nectar that they obtain by hovering in place and probing their bills into a flower's center. When hovering, they stroke their wings over 50 times a second, producing a low humming sound as they maneuver forward, backward, sideways, and up and down. Favored flowers are tubular, and red to orange in color, including jewelweed, trumpet creeper, snapdragons, and columbine.

Hummingbirds serve as pollinators when moving from flower to flower. They appear to remember which flowers they have visited most recently and will not return to it until its nectar has been replenished. In addition to nectar, Ruby-throated Hummingbirds eat tiny insects, spiders, and larvae that they find in flowers, and they catch insects such as gnats in mid-air. Seemingly fearless, these exciting birds can be easily attracted with hummingbird feeders. Quarrels at feeders result in darting chases exceeding 30 miles per hour, during which wings whine and the birds squeak and twitter.

Ruby-throated Hummingbirds are the only regularly expected hummingbirds in the eastern half of the United States. They return to their nesting grounds in late April and early May. Nests are made of lichens and spider web strands and usually situated high in trees, often over streams or lake shores. They are nearly impossible to find as they are saddled on a limb, only two inches across and camouflaged with bits of lichen. Their two white eggs are no bigger than peanuts. The young hatch in two weeks and fly from the nest three weeks later. This species nests twice a summer.

Late summer numbers are bolstered by the addition of the new young, which resemble females. By late September, most Ruby-throats have departed for Mexico and Central America. Some cross the Gulf of Mexico in a single, 500-mile flight.

## IDENTIFICATION TIPS

▶ perched, it is big-headed and big-billed; larger than a Robin

▶ blue-gray above, with a ragged bushy crest and a broad gray breast band

▶ female has an additional rusty breast band

▶ hovers on rapidly-beating wings before diving

▶ seen singly or in pairs along streams and ponds

▶ has deep, irregular wingbeats in flight

▶ loud rattling call

▶ except for terns, kingfishers are the only small birds that dive headfirst into water

# BELTED KINGFISHER
*Ceryle alcyon*

hese heavily-built, foot-long birds perch in the open along streams and lake shores. They are easily recognized by their large, crested heads, bluish-gray upper-parts, and their white bellies with the blue chest-bands that give them their name. Females have an additional belt of brown. In flight, they emit a loud, rattling call. Their wing-beats are deep and irregular.

Belted Kingfishers prefer clear water so that they can spy fish swimming just beneath the surface. They sometimes hover at heights of up to 30 feet before dropping bill first into the water. Often it is the splash that first attracts a person's attention. Catches are usually small fish that are carried to a perch in the bill. Holding the fish by the tail, the bird swings its head repeatedly against the perch, stunning it before swallowing it headfirst.

Belted Kingfishers range across North America. They migrate south in winter to areas of open water and back north in spring, nesting in all but the hottest and driest regions of the country. Nests are excavated in vertical banks of soil, usually in riverbanks. Burrow entrances can sometimes be spotted by boaters. They are two to three feet below the top of the bank, four inches in diameter, and have two tracks at the bottom resulting from the bird's feet. A tunnel extends upward from the entrance for a short distance and then back into the bank as far as ten feet before terminating in a spherical egg chamber about 12-inches in diameter.

Here the female lays her four to five white eggs, in April or May. They hatch following 22 to 24 days of incubation and the young depart the burrow about a month later. Belted Kingfishers nest once a year.

**IDENTIFICATION TIPS**

▶ black and white "ladder" barring on back; red cap and white rump

▶ red covers crown and nape in male, but only nape in female

▶ juvenile is also ladder-backed, but has a brown head that shows no red

# RED-BELLIED WOODPECKER

*Melanerpes carolinus*

hese nine-inch woodpeckers are well known to the south of New York State. Despite not ranging through the entire East, they are included in this book because, where they do occur, they are well-known. They are expanding their range northward, perhaps because of their inclination to visit bird feeders stocked with sunflower seeds. Red-bellied Woodpeckers have black-and-white cross-barring on their backs, and red caps. The red extends completely over the top of a male's head, whereas the top of a female's head is gray. The name "Red-bellied" is mystifying unless a bird is examined closely. Though there is a rose wash on the tummy, it seems inconceivable that those who named this species could not have come up with a better name.

Because Red-bellied Woodpeckers are able to drill wood-boring beetles and larvae from wood in winter as well as summer, they are nonmigratory throughout most of their range. In addition, they eat various nuts, fruits, and seeds, especially from fall through spring. Their most familiar call, which can be heard at any season, is a trilling *churr*. Beginning in spring, especially in response to nearby members of the opposite sex, both males and females emit *ta-wik - ta-wik - ta-wik* calls. Loud drumming, which is another courtship sound, is delivered in bursts lasting about one second.

From April through July, Red-bellied Woodpeckers excavate holes measuring about two inches in diameter in the decayed tops of trees. Cavities are about one foot deep. Like most eggs sheltered in darkness, the eggs require no concealing coloration, so they are white. The four to five eggs hatch in 11 days, and the young leave the cavity 24 to 26 days later. Red-bellied Woodpeckers raise two broods in the south and one in the north. As typical of woodpeckers, Red-bellieds excavate a new cavity with each nesting. This is important ecologically as old cavities secondarily provide habitat for a variety of cavity-nesting wildlife, ranging from bluebirds to chickadees to flying squirrels.

## IDENTIFICATION TIPS

▶ finely mottled back and narrow, longish white wing strip are diagnostic

▶ red forehead patch; male has red throat patch; female has a white throat

▶ sapsuckers tap in distinctive rhythms but do not drum

# Yellow-bellied Sapsucker

*Sphyrapicus varius*

hough the name of this specialized woodpecker may be humorous, it is fitting because of their diet. Yellow-bellied Sapsuckers feed on tree sap by drilling shallow parallel rows of small holes into soft inner bark, and using their brush-like tongue to lap it up. They visit these sap wells repeatedly until they run dry, also consuming insects that the sap attracts. Birds such as Yellow-rumped Warblers and Ruby-throated Hummingbrids also visit the sapsucker holes, the latter often relying on them when their spring arrival precedes the major emergence of blossoms.

The feeding holes made by Yellow-bellied Sapsuckers are easily recognized, and actually more often seen than their reclusive architects. Those in deciduous trees are often round, about one-fourth-inch in diameter, and aligned horizontally, sometimes encircling the trunk. Those in evergreens are often closely grouped squares, each about one-half-inch wide. If liquid sap is still in the well, a sapsucker is likely to be somewhere nearby. These eight-inch birds have black and white barring on the back, wings, and tail, like many of the woodpecker family. They have a black bib and a light-yellow wash on the breast. There is a patch of scarlet on the forehead. Males have scarlet throats, whereas females have white throats. A longish white patch in the wing is best seen on flying birds. They emit low *mews* and *kee-yews*, especially during the spring.

Yellow-bellied Sapsuckers nest through much of the northeastern United States and to the south in the Appalachian Mountains. Nesting cavities are excavated by both sexes and sometimes used for several years. They lay four to seven white eggs, which hatch in 12 to 13 days. The young depart the cavity in about three weeks. Immature Yellow-bellied Sapsuckers are so brown-streaked that they are often mistaken as dirty (they do show the white patch on the wing, however). Though migratory, Yellow-bellied Sapsuckers inhabit much of the East in winter.

## IDENTIFICATION TIPS

► white back; small, slender bill
► small edition of the Hairy Woodpecker, which is larger and has a large bill
► barred outer tail feathers are diagnostic
► may be mistaken for a Yellow-bellied Sapsucker, whose white stripe is on the wing, not the back; sapsucker's belly is yellow

# DOWNY WOODPECKER

*Picoides pubescens*

These common, six-inch woodpeckers are tiny compared to their relatives. Black and white, like most woodpeckers, their only brilliance is a spot of red at the back of the head — present in males only. They are nearly identical to Hairy Woodpeckers (*Picoides villosus*), who likewise are distributed nearly throughout the North American continent. Hairy Woodpeckers, however, are less common, nearly two inches longer, have bills nearly as long as their heads, and their white outer tail feathers are pure white. Downy Woodpeckers have bills much shorter than their heads, and their white tail feathers are flecked with black. The two species even sound similar, emitting a single *pik* or a long, descending rattle.

Downy Woodpeckers can be seen at any time of year in suburban yards, mixed woodlands, and even cultivated areas. Their size enables them to work small twigs and stems that are out of the reach of their larger relatives. They consume wood-boring beetles, larvae, ants, and in the fall, can be seen extracting borers from corn stalks or hammering apart an insect gall on a goldenrod stem. They also visit feeding stations for seeds and suet.

Courtship drumming and pairing commence in late winter but actual nesting does not usually get underway until May. Nesting cavities are excavated in the dead parts of trees, frequently just beneath a broken-off top. The parents take turns incubating the four to six pure white eggs. Incubation requires 12 days, and the young fly form the nest cavity at 20 to 23 days of age. Their parents feed them for another two weeks before initiating a second nesting.

Like other woodpeckers, Downy Woodpeckers have a long, barbed tongue for extracting insects from deep in wood. It can project the length of the bill beyond the bill-tip. For the necessary elasticity, a woodpecker's tongue extends through the back of the skull beneath the skin, over the top of the head, and is anchored near a nostril.

**IDENTIFICATION TIPS**

▶ jay sized with brown back, no white on the wings, and a black breast crescent

▶ in flight, the white rump is conspicuous; yellow under wings and tail

▶ often hop awkwardly on the ground; flight is deeply undulating

# NORTHERN FLICKER
*Colaptes auratus*

hese large, common woodpeckers often eat ants on or near the ground. Especially during their spring and fall migrations, when one is seen, there are likely others scattered about the lawn or forest floor. They are 11 inches long and the only North American woodpeckers to be primarily brown rather than black and white. They have white rumps, black bibs, and spotted breasts. Those that live from the Great Plains to the East Coast have wing and tail feathers with vivid yellow patterns. This contributes to a yellow underwing that can be seen in flight. The identifiable yellow-shafted feathers are sometimes noticed on the ground during the late-summer molt.

Typical of woodpeckers in flight, Northern Flickers alternate between flapping and tucking their wings, resulting in an undulating, roller-coaster flight. Their call is a prolonged *wicka . . . wicka . . . wicka*, primarily given as the birds are pairing-up in spring. A courting pair performs a dance involving the spreading of wings and tail while emitting a slow *cha . . . weeka . . . cha . . . weeka* in unison. Males have black "moustaches" at the corner of their bills, whereas females have none. The male is the primary excavator of the nesting cavity, typically in the trunks of dead trees. Entrances are roundish, about three-and-a-half inches in diameter, and most often face to the east or south. The nest chamber continues down into the tree trunk another foot. It is lined with wood chips for the six to eight white eggs. The eggs hatch in 11 days and the young exit the nest cavity 24 to 27 days later.

In addition to ants, Northern Flickers eat a variety of insects that they chisel from trees, as well as berries and seeds. They sometimes visit bird feeding stations for sunflower seeds and suet. Though Northern Flickers migrate short distances, they live year-round across most of the United States.

### IDENTIFICATION TIPS

▶ great size; solid black back; flaming red crest
▶ sweeping wingbeats and flashing white under wing areas identify the Pileated in flight
▶ large oval or oblong holes in dead trees indicate its presence
▶ call is a series, never single

# PILEATED WOODPECKER

*Dryocopus pileatus*

With the disappearance of Ivory-billed Woodpeckers (*Campephilus principalis*), these are the largest and most dramatic woodpeckers remaining in North America. At 15 inches in length, they are nearly as large as crows. The diagnostic flaming red crest is present on both sexes, but the male of the pair is identified by a red "moustache" whereas the female's is black. Additionally, the female has a black forehead. When flying overhead, they sail directly and with seeming effortlessness, their broad wings nearly closing with each deep stroke. Their loud, rapid *wuk wuk wuk wuk* call rings through the woods at any season and has such a wild quality as to be used as recorded background sounds in jungle movies. It has been described as a laugh and, although the cartoon version of their sound is rather inaccurate, these birds were the model for "Woody the Woodpecker."

Many people erroneously believe that these birds are rare or even endangered. Pileated Woodpeckers rarely stray from the deep woods and are especially associated with the huge trees of river floodplains. They range through forested landscapes from the East Coast westward to the plains and through the mixed coniferous and deciduous forests of the North through Canada to the Pacific Northwest. Where they do reside, they are year-round residents.

These impressive woodpeckers eat mostly wood boring beetles and larvae. Using their heavy, three-inch bill to alternately hammer, pry, and rip, whole portions of a rotting tree can be splintered apart in a matter of seconds. The underlying morsels are nabbed up with a tongue that projects well beyond the bill. They also eat grains and nuts. Pileated Woodpeckers can sometimes be attracted to feeding stations that offer suet.

These large woodpeckers pair for life. Nesting cavities are excavated in trunks of large trees in spring. The oval entrance is about three inches wide by four inches high. By May, the parents are exchanging incubation duties. There is an average of four white eggs. They hatch in 18 days. The young leave the nest cavity about a month later.

## IDENTIFICATION TIPS

▶ sparrow-sized
▶ similar to the Eastern Phoebe, but with 2 narrow white wing bars and a light lower beak
▶ lack of contrast between head and back
▶ no eye ring
▶ usually do not wag their tails
▶ immature Eastern Phoebes have buffy wing bars in fall, but their breasts are lemon yellow

# EASTERN WOOD-PEWEE

*Contopus virens*

astern Wood-Pewees are rather small, nondescript flycatchers that are more often heard than seen. They live in deciduous forests in the eastern half of North America. Named for their song, they emit a high, thin *pee-ah-wee* that wafts through the woods on late spring and summer days. Through diligence, the singer can usually be sighted, typically perched on a bare limb in the forest mid-story. Their relatively large, crowned heads identify them as flycatchers. Eastern Wood-Pewees are five-and-a-quarter inches in length and are dark gray above and lighter gray below. The presence of wing-bars distinguishes them from Eastern Phoebes

Eastern Wood-Pewees are one of the latest migrants to return in spring, having traveled from South America. Their appearance in May coincides with a major emergence of flying insects. Like other flycatchers, Eastern Wood-Pewees take insects during short flights, returning to the same perch again and again. Their cup nests are built well out on the upper surface of a horizontal branch and covered with lichens until indistinguishable from knots. The Eastern Wood-Pewee's eggs are white with wreaths of purple spots. There are two to five eggs in a clutch. They hatch after 13 days of incubation. It may require another two weeks for the young to depart the nest. Despite the Eastern Wood-Pewee's abundance, little else is known of their reproductive behavior, including whether or not they nest more than once a season.

## IDENTIFICATION TIPS

► tail-bobbing is diagnostic
► solid black bill
► gray-brown; sparrow-sized; dark head (darker than back; head of Eastern Wood-Pewee is same shade as back)
► no eye ring or strong wing bars
► immatures can be mistaken for pewees because of their dull wing bars

# EASTERN PHOEBE

*Sayornis phoebe*

lthough simply small, dark birds, Eastern Phoebes attract attention. Foremost, they tend to live near people, especially in rural areas, nesting on porches, in out-buildings, and under eaves, decks, and docks. At six-inches in length, they are dark gray above and light below. Like other members of their flycatcher family, they have the hint of a crest on their head, but unlike most flycatchers, they lack wing-bars, except for first year birds. Their best identifier is the manner in which they continually bob their tail up and down, and their raspy, atonal *fee-bee* calls. This sound can be heard immediately upon the Eastern Phoebe's return in March and continues through much of the summer.

Eastern Phoebes are remarkably solitary. Although monogamous, seldom is more than one seen at the same time, even when nesting. The female alone constructs the nest where it will be sheltered from above, often along streams, under rock ledges and bridges, but also on buildings. The four-inch wide by four-inch high nest is composed of varying amounts of mud, depending on the need for it to adhere to a surface. It is covered with moss and lined with fine grasses, feathers, and hair. It may take a week or two for a nest to be completed and then it may sit empty for another week before receiving its first egg, usually in early April. Typical clutches contain five eggs. The eggs are milky white. They hatch in 16 days. The young fledge 16 days later.

The parents fall silent while nesting, but as their youngsters fledge, the adults resume calling in preparation for another nesting. Previous nests are renovated or new nests constructed for the second and final family of the year. These young typically take flight in July. Following a late summer molt, Eastern Phoebes depart in September for their winter range. Eastern Phoebes nest from the East Coast to the Great Plains, and winter from the southern states through northern Mexico.

# GREAT CRESTED FLYCATCHER
*Myiarchus crinitus*

sually the first clue that a Great Crested Flycatcher is around is the loud, ascending *wheeeeep* call coming from the tree tops. This noisy flycatcher is still hard to pick out among the foliage. Its yellow underside is often glimpsed first, and then the rusty color of the wings and tail as it flits among the branches. More careful observation will discern the gray throat and breast, and the flycatcher family's trademark crown.

Although only seven inches long, Great Crested Flycatchers are the largest and most observable of our woodland flycatchers. Having wintered from Mexico to Venezuela, they return to nest in May, just when the tender, new leaves begin to support high numbers of insects. They glean bugs and worms from leaves, and make short flights to take moths and flies from the air. They inhabit woodland edges and the scattered trees of parks, pastures, and suburban yards from the East Coast to the Rocky Mountains.

Cavity nesters, they typically choose holes produced when branches have broken off of dead trees. Occasionally they use man-made structures such as mailboxes and bird houses. Their relatively large clutches of up to eight eggs hatch in about 15 days. The young fledge in another 15 days. They nest once and are on their way south by the end of August.

Great Crested Flycatchers often locate shed snake skins to place in their nesting cavities, together with their nesting material. This may deter cavity nesting competitors and predators who recognize snakes as threats. Cavities containing snake skins tend to be avoided by mice and flying squirrels, known predators of eggs and nestlings.

# EASTERN KINGBIRD
*Tyrannus tyrannus*

These open-country birds are the most conspicuous flycatchers in the East. They are most likely seen perched on fence wires or utility lines along rural roads. At eight inches in length, they are immaculate white below and dark charcoal above. The best identifier is a white band completely across the tip of the tail, present in no other North American songbird. Their heads are slightly crested, as is characteristic of members of the flycatcher family. The narrow red streak down the middle of the crown is seldom noticed. Their call is an emphatic *bzzzzt*.

As is typical of flycatchers, Eastern Kingbirds feed by making short, sallying flights from perches. They snatch insects as large as grasshoppers from the air. Bees and wasps constitute such a large portion of their diet that in some places they are known as "bee martins." Their common name, "kingbird," stems from their commanding relationship with other birds. Acting individually or as pairs, they fearlessly drive birds as large as hawks from their premises with repeated dives and actual physical contact. Their Latin name, *Tyrannus*, meaning "tyrant," also originates from this domineering manner.

Eastern Kingbirds breed throughout the Atlantic States and westward through the Great Plains. Having wintered in South America, they arrive back on their breeding grounds in late April and early May. Pairing ensues and nest building commences in June. Although nesting areas are typically open fields, Eastern Kingbirds require a few trees in which to build their nests. Most nests are situated well out on a limb and so bulky that they can quite easily be seen when looking up through the branches. The two to five white, brown-spotted eggs hatch in 15 days, and the young fledge 17 days later, usually in early July. They nest only once a season. Their relatively low reproductive rate is countered by prolonged parental care following fledging, which improves the survival of young.

## IDENTIFICATION TIPS

▶ blue-gray cap contrasts with olive back
▶ strong, white eyebrow stripe is bordered
  by black
▶ red iris is not obvious at a distance
▶ song repeated as often as 40 times per
  minute, and typically continues for many
  minutes without a long break

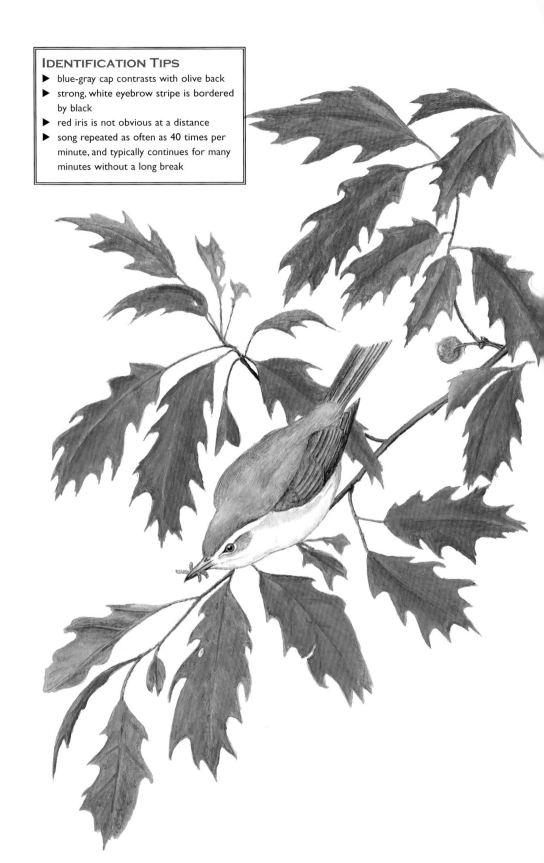

# RED-EYED VIREO

*Vireo olivaceus*

hese are North America's most vocal birds. Their song is Robin-like, except divided by short pauses into sweet, clear phrases resembling *cheeree..cheeryup..cheerwit*. It can be heard from within almost any substantial woods between April and July from the break of day through the heat of the afternoon. A single individual is reported to have sung an amazing 22,197 times within a ten hour period.

Despite nearly everyone having heard these common forest birds at one time or another, few have taken the time to pick out their song from among the various melodies emanating from the woods. Red-eyed Vireos are not as lively as wood warblers; people who make the effort are often able to study an individual with binoculars as it hunts through the foliage. In addition to their surprisingly red eyes, these five-and-a-half inch olive songbirds have a white and black stripe above the eye. They are otherwise rather plain and lack wing-bars. The sexes are alike. Those younger than a year have dark rather than red irises.

Vireos, in general, have relatively heavy bills that have tiny hooks at the tip for picking caterpillars and crawling insects from leaves and twigs. Having wintered in the Amazon Basin, Red-eyed Vireos return to their North American range in April. Their arrival coincides with the emergence of new, succulent leaves, which are especially inviting to their insect prey. They weave nests of grasses and fibers that hang from their brims in the forks of lateral branches. In this way, their nests are similar to those of orioles, but shallower.

Red-eyed Vireos typically lay a clutch of four eggs. They usually raise two families a year, beginning in May and ending in July. No bird species is more heavily parasitized by Brown-headed Cowbirds. Despite this handicap, Red-eyed Vireos remain common residents of our deciduous forests.

# BLUE JAY
*Cyanocitta cristata*

onspicuous and fascinating to watch, Blue Jays exhibit many of the characteristics of their crow relatives. Nearly everyone from the East through the Midwest knows these common, ten-inch-long birds. People who feed birds often get the chance to witness their sociality. A few bird watchers disapprove of the Blue Jay's gang-like aggressiveness, and their opinion of them is further reduced when they learn that Blue Jays tend to prey on the eggs and nestlings of other birds. The Blue Jays, of course, are only behaving as designed by the forces of natural selection, and it is unfair to evaluate them with human standards.

Members of the crow family, in general, are renowned for their intelligence, and the Blue Jay's large vocal repertoire provides a hint of their surprising intellect. It has been suggested that they communicate with as many as 21 different sounds, each with a distinct meaning. Included in this "language" is the commonly heard *jay* call, which gives them their name. It is reminiscent of a jeer and, fittingly, is used to muster Blue Jays in the mobbing of perceived threats. "Pump-handle" or "bell" calls are accompanied by the pumping of the body and function to alert the others. Females greet other females with "rattle" calls as they assemble in trees. Jays also emit *peeps*, *clucks*, and "whisper songs," delivered when in close proximity to each other, thus resembling conversation.

Blue Jays migrate in fall to where foods such as acorns are available. Despite this movement, they reside in most of their summer range throughout the year. Monogamous, with sexes identical, pairs become silent when near their nests, which are well-hidden in trees. Nests are made of sticks and are about nine inches across. Clutches are laid in April and May. They usually contain four to five eggs, which are greenish-buff and speckled. The female incubates the eggs and they hatch in 17 to 18 days. The young leave the nest at around 17 days of age, before fully capable of flight.

Blue Jays are omnivorous, eating a wide variety of animal and plant material. This trait, plus their remarkable intelligence, has allowed them to thrive despite environmental changes caused by humans. Blue Jays that visit bird feeders often arrive as a group and behave warily. They may swallow as many as 20 sunflower seeds whole before flying to a safe location to spit them out. They then crack them open one by one while holding them under their toes.

## IDENTIFICATION TIPS

▶ male is uniformly blue-black all over (no other swallow is dark all over)
▶ female is light-bellied; throat and breast grayish, often with a faint collar above
▶ glides in circles; often spreads tail
▶ largest North American swallow

♀

♂

# PURPLE MARTIN

*Progne subis*

These eight-inch swallows are named for the glossy, deep blue plumage of the males. Females and males younger than two years are brownish with light bellies and, if it were not for their larger size, might be confused with other swallows. Like other members of their family, Purple Martins catch insects from the air during extended flights. Unlike their smaller relatives, however, they tend to forage higher and on larger prey. Foods include airborne beetles, flies, moths, wasps, dragonflies, grasshoppers, and insects as large as cicadas.

Purple Martins are unique among birds in that throughout most of their range they nest only in homes provided specifically for them by humans. Once tree cavity nesters, they took to man-made quarters so readily that by 1900, they rarely nested in natural sites. Many people around the country invite colonies to their yards with specially-designed martin houses. The liquid twittering of Purple Martins perched along wires, and their graceful, sweeping flight overhead add a decorative feature to a neighborhood. Additionally, many Purple Martin land-lords attest that their birds consume volumes of insect pests.

Males arrive on the breeding grounds in March, preceding females by a week to ten days. This is surprisingly early and potentially hazardous considering their dependency on flying insects. An early arrival is a worthwhile gamble, however, as it enables them to claim the most desirable nesting sites. Nesting begins in May. A clutch of four to five white eggs hatches in 15 days and the young fly a month later. Martins nest once a season in the northern part of their range and twice in the south. They breed from the East Coast through the Great Plains and sparingly through the Desert Southwest and along the West Coast.

After rearing of young is completed, in July, Purple Martins begin perching on power lines in neighborhoods as they prepare for their remarkable journey south. These flocks gradually coalesce with others until there may be immense flocks of thousands in only a few locales. By late August, they have vanished and are well on their way to their distant winter range. They winter east of the Andes in South America, often as huge flocks in cities such as Sao Paulo, Brazil.

## IDENTIFICATION TIPS

▶ green-blue/black on back, clear white below

▶ glides in circles; ends each glide with 3 or 4 quick flaps and a short climb

▶ immature has dusky brown back and incomplete breastband; easy to confuse with Rough-winged Swallow (it has a dingier throat), or Bank Swallow (it has a complete breast band); Tree Swallow's throat is always white

# TREE SWALLOW

*Tachycineta bicolor*

hese five-inch-long swallows gleam with metallic greens and blues depending on the angle of light. They are immaculate white below and their tails are shallowly forked. Where one is seen, there are usually several, each darting and swooping independently after airborne insects over ponds and meadows. Though most swallow species shun trees to an extent, Tree Swallows readily perch in them, befitting their name. They also nest in tree cavities, especially in dead trees near water that have been hollowed out by woodpeckers.

Tree Swallows breed across North America with the exception of the deep south, the arid west, and the treeless tundra of the far north. Generally, they are most numerous in cooler, damper climates. They return from Mexico and Central America to various latitudes of their breeding range between late March and early May. Their arrival proceeds egg laying by several weeks because, as with Purple Martins, an early return is an advantage in competing for appropriate nesting sites. Perhaps because of nest cavity competition, Tree Swallows often use man-made nest boxes, occasionally occupying those intended for bluebirds.

Tree Swallows construct a cup of fine grasses at the base of the cavity and then proceed to line it with downy feathers that they find scattered about. Males collect the nest material and are sometimes so desperate for feathers that they swoop close by to catch those that people toss into the air for them. Over 100 feathers have been counted in a single nest. The female assembles the material and alone incubates the four to six glossy white eggs for the two week incubation period. Both parents feed the young for 15 to 25 days while in the nest. As the young near their fledging date, the parents must work feverishly to keep them fed.

Young Tree Swallows can be seen flying with adults as early as June. They are brown in place of green until the following spring, and are difficult to distinguish from other swallows. Tree Swallows nest only once each year.

# NORTHERN ROUGH-WINGED SWALLOW
### *Stelgidopteryx serripennis*

These are the quintessential little brown birds. There are few swallow-like birds so dully-colored except female and immature Purple Martins, which are substantially larger. At five-and-a-half inches in length, Northern Rough-winged Swallows are simply brown above with dusky throats and breasts grading to white on the belly. Although recognizable as swallows from their continuous flight and long, swept back wings, they are otherwise so indistinguishable as to be named for the rough texture of the outer primary quill.

Northern Rough-winged Swallows consume flying insects, typically over lakes, rivers, and meadows. They characteristically cruise swiftly within a foot or two of the grass or water's surface, then swoop upward to change direction before another low pass. Usually several will forage in the same area though not necessarily together. Feeding may continue for hours with the birds rarely taking time to land. When they do roost, it is usually with their own kind. They select thin, open perches such as the tips of bare branches or utility wires. Typical of swallows, their feet are designed for perching rather than walking.

Northern Rough-winged Swallows return from the tropics in early April and spread across the Lower 48 States. Nesting occurs where there are existing holes such crevices in rock ledges or burrows in earthen banks. Highway travelers often see them flittering about the faces of road-cuts. Where several crevices occur together, Rough-winged Swallows will form small nesting colonies. Grass and stems are used to construct a cup for the clutch of four to six white eggs. They hatch in 16 days. The young wait until able to fly well before departing the nest, at around 20 days of age, in late June or early July. There is only one nesting each summer. Large flocks assemble in September when preparing for the fall migration.

## IDENTIFICATION TIPS

▶ rusty orange rump, square tail, broad wings, buff-colored forehead

▶ overhead, the bird appears square-tailed, with a dark throat patch

▶ glides in a long eclipse, ending each glide with a steep climb

▶ soars more than other swallows

# CLIFF SWALLOW
*Petrochelidon pyrrhonota*

ike other swallows, Cliff Swallows are readily seen because they feed on airborne flies out in the open. What makes them even more conspicuous, however, is the fact that there are so many of them. Because they are colonial, people tend to see none or many, but if a total tally of their numbers were possible, they might prove to be the most abundant bird species in North America. Their abundance is partly due to their huge breeding range, which extends from Alaska through all but the most arid regions of the west and nearly to the East Coast. Within this domain, they form large colonies, some containing as many as 3,500 nesting pairs.

These standard-sized swallows are about five inches in length and readily identified by their orange rumps, easily seen when in flight. Their tail is squared-off, rather than forked, and they have a spot of buff on the forehead. The sexes are alike. They emit a melodious, purring call as they fly about.

Though distributed widely today, up until the mid-1800s, Cliff Swallows were restricted to the mountainous west where they constructed their unique, funnel-shaped, mud nests beneath rocky ledges. A lack of cliffs on the Great Plains prevented them from expanding their range into eastern North America until humans constructed bridges, a suitable substitute for cliffs, throughout the plains. Now that Cliff Swallows have bridged that gap, they have colonized much of the eastern half of the continent where they sometimes have reverted to nest on natural sites. They were first recorded in New York State in 1817 and their numbers improved until the early 1900s when the removal of old barns, a common nesting site, and competition with House Sparrows, who take over nests, may have reduced their nesting success.

Throughout most of the eastern United States, Cliff Swallows nest primarily on manmade structures, including buildings, bridges, culverts, and dams. Colonies sometimes resemble numerous mud jugs packed closely together. The first and only brood is raised from May through July. Incubation of the two to six speckled eggs requires two weeks and rearing another two. In September, Cliff Swallows form huge flocks of many thousands in preparation for migration. They winter in South America.

# BARN SWALLOW
*Hirundo rustica*

**B**arn Swallows are denizens of rural landscapes across North America. They are so associated with the countryside that their scientific name, *rustica*, means "of the country" in Latin. These sleek, six-inch swallows are exquisitely designed for continuous flight and high maneuverability because of their swept-back wings and deeply-forked tails. Where one is seen, there are typically others, cruising swiftly within a few feet of the ground over pastures or near herds of cattle, capturing the flying insects that compose their diet. Or they will sweep deftly into open barn doors or hover in place, often while twittering constantly.

Barn Swallows return in early April but do not usually begin nesting until May. Because their nests are made from mud, they must be situated where protected from rain. Barns, other open buildings, bridges, and porches are usual sites, especially if there is suitable mud in the vicinity at the time of construction. Both members of the pair carry beads of mud in their bills and plaster it to the side of a rafter or similar structure, forming a half-cup. The mud is strengthened with interwoven straw. Fine straw is used to line the nest, as are poultry feathers to warm and cushion the eggs. Nest construction can take a week.

Clutches contain four to six eggs, which are white with brown speckles. They require 14 days of incubation, and the young fly from the nest at 20 days of age. Where conditions are favorable, several pairs will nest together. As many as 50 nests have been reported in a single barn. Nests are reused to raise another brood, typically in July.

Following the nesting period, adults and new young perch along power lines near farmsteads throughout the countryside. As fall sets in, they coalesce into fewer but larger flocks, containing thousands. They migrate by day, beginning in September. The Barn Swallow's wintering range extends from Panama to the tip of South America. They also occur throughout Europe, Africa, and Asia, and are one of the world's most widespread birds.

## IDENTIFICATION TIPS
▶ tiny; black cap and bib with white cheeks
▶ sides are buff-colored

# BLACK-CAPPED CHICKADEE
*Poecile atricapillus*

These four-and-a-half inch packets of energy are among North America's best known birds. They are common wherever mature trees predominate, whether in cities or the country. Their song is a clear, two- to three-noted whistle with the first note the highest. They are permanent residents and singing can commence soon after the first of the year. Their scold is the sassy *chick-a-dee-dee* that gives them their name. Chickadees can easily be attracted to bird feeders with sunflower seeds and suet. Feeders designed to exclude large birds, such as mesh bags, are easily mastered by them because of their ability to land and cling on vertical surfaces or even upside down. They employ the same acrobatics to pick insects from branches and seeds from seed heads.

Black-capped Chickadees excavate nesting cavities in rotting wood or use abandoned woodpecker holes and bird houses. Nests are made of moss and plant fibers, and lined with hair and feathers. Only the female incubates the large clutch of five to ten white, speckled eggs. She is regularly fed by her mate during this two-week period. The young are fed by both parents during the two weeks that they are growing in the nest and up to a month after leaving the cavity. Nesting takes place from April through June. In some areas, a second nesting may follow the first.

Black-capped Chickadees are permanent residents throughout New England southward through Pennsylvania, then down the higher elevations of the Appalachian Mountains. Despite weighing only one-third ounce, they are able to survive temperatures of minus 50 degrees Fahrenheit. To conserve energy during severe cold, they fluff their feathers, tuck up their legs, and lower their body temperature by up to 20 degrees.

At the southern terminus of their range, the nearly identical Carolina Chickadee (*Poecile carolinensis*) takes over. Carolina Chickadees inhabit the lower elevations from Pennsylvania southward. Where the two chickadee species' ranges meet, they do not overlap. Though difficult to distinguish visually, Carolina Chickadees have a four-parted whistled song that is up-down-up-down in tone. A third Chickadee, the Boreal Chickadee (*Poecile hudsonica*) shares the range of the Black-capped Chickadee from the Adirondacks through northern Vermont, New Hampshire, and Maine. It is identified by its brownish plumage.

**IDENTIFICATION TIPS**
- ▶ small, gray, mouse-colored; rust-colored flanks
- ▶ tufted crest
- ▶ usually found in flocks of 3-8 birds

# TUFTED TITMOUSE

*Baeolophus bicolor*

These five-and-a-half inch, gray, crested songbirds are residents of deciduous forests of the southeastern states. They fade out to the north of Pennsylvania and Connecticut. Where they do occur, they are familiar, primarily because of the ease that they are attracted to bird feeders. In fact, there is some evidence that they are expanding their range northward because of the increasing popularity of this hobby. Like their relatives the chickadees, Tufted Titmice are able to cling and dangle from feeders to select preferred seeds. They especially favor sunflower seeds which they hold beneath their toes to hammer open with their bills. Those kernels not immediately swallowed are flown to nearby trees to be pressed between furrows of bark, presumably to be consumed later.

Tufted Titmice are permanent residents throughout their range. A pair may reside in the same few acres throughout life. Especially at the onset of the breeding season, from February through April, their loud *peter-peter-peter* calls echo through the woodland from every direction. Due to their strong defense of nesting territories, males can sometimes be lured into view with even pathetic imitations of their whistled songs. Annoyed by what they perceive to be an intruder, they switch to a sassy, low *tsk-dee-dee*.

Tufted Titmice nest in woodpecker holes, bird houses and other cavities, forming a cup of grass, shredded bark, and leaves. Titmice are sometimes so desperate to collect hair to line their nests that they pull it from neighborhood dogs, passing deer, and even human heads. Eggs are laid in April. Clutches may contain as many as nine eggs, which are white and sparingly spotted. Incubation requires 12 to 14 days. The young fledge at 17 or 18 days of age, usually in May.

## IDENTIFICATION TIPS

▶ climbs down trees head-first
▶ black cap is grayer in females
▶ white face with small black eyes

# WHITE-BREASTED NUTHATCH

*Sitta carolinensis*

The *yank-yank-yank* voice of the White-breasted Nuthatch is common in oak-hickory woods in winter as well as summer. These five-inch, black, gray and white birds are the only tree climbers able to move head-first down tree trunks. This enables them to find insects in the bark that might be missed by "tree-up" gleaners such as woodpeckers. In addition to insects, they eat seeds that they press into crevices in bark and hack open with their bills. Early observers noticed this behavior and used it in their name. They often visit bird feeders, especially relishing sunflower seeds.

An adult pair will spend its entire life within a 25 to 50 acre patch of woods. Nuthatches nest in tree holes originally excavated by woodpeckers. Egg-laying commences from late April through May. They have surprisingly large clutches of up to ten eggs. Due to the protection afforded by the cavity, like other cavity nesters, White-breasted Nuthatches will rear nearly all of their young if food is available. Families are raised by July. There is no subsequent nesting during the year.

The sexes of White-breasted Nuthatches are nearly alike except for the male's blacker crown. To add a bit of confusion, there is a second nuthatch, the Red-breasted Nuthatch (*Sitta canadensis*), that breeds in northern coniferous forests from New York State through Maine. It migrates south in winter to occupy the entire East region. Red-breasted Nuthatches are slightly smaller and, as suggested by their name, their breasts are tinged with red. They are best distinguished from White-breasted Nuthatches by a black stripe through the eye. Wintering birds continue to display an affinity for pines. They also visit bird feeders.

- large wren, about the size of a small sparrow
- ▶ warm rufous-brown above, bright buff-colored below
- ▶ conspicuous eyebrow stripe

# CAROLINA WREN

*Thryothorus ludovicianus*

arolina Wrens exhibit the usual wren characteristics of a roundish body, fine bill, and cocked tail. These wrens, however, are rusty with vivid, white eye-lines. And, although small, they are the largest wrens in the eastern United States. At five inches in length and seven ounces, they are double the weight of House Wrens. Carolina Wrens are well-known in the southeastern United States, south of a line extending from western Pennsylvania through Long Island. Their numbers diminish to the north of that line and they are essentially absent from all but the southern parts of New York and Massachusetts. They are non-migrating, permanent residents throughout their range.

Although distributed through only a portion of the East, Carolina Wrens are included in this book because, where they do reside, they are often encountered. For rural residents within their range, Carolina Wrens are especially familiar because they frequent gardens and shrubs, and tend to build nests in farm implements, stored boats, firewood stacks, mail boxes, and hanging flower pots. People who are attentive to their ringing *tea kettle - tea kettle - tea kettle* call, hear them at all seasons and sometimes in the woods well away from human habitation.

Having occupied nesting territories through the winter, Carolina Wren pairs begin nest construction in March. Composed of grass, leaves, and feathers, these bulky structures are situated where protected from the weather. A typical clutch contains four to six eggs. The eggs are white with encircling speckles of brown. Incubation requires 15 days, and the young depart the nest at 12 to 14 days of age. Carolina Wrens nest as many as three times until as late September.

Because they are largely insectivorous and year-round residents, Carolina Wren numbers are sometimes reduced by severe winter weather. On cold winter nights, people sometimes find them fluffed into unrecognizable puff balls under awnings and in sheds.

# HOUSE WREN

*Troglodytes aedon*

ecause of their affinity for yards and gardens, House Wrens are one of America's best known birds, ranging from coast to coast. At a mere four-and-a-half inches in length, they are tiny packets of energy. Quivering, they burst forth with their bubbling, chattering songs usually from a perch within a few feet of the ground. Despite their usual boisterousness, they can become quiet when skulking through bushes and undergrowth hunting the small insects that constitute the majority of their diet. Only when there is a perceived danger, such as a human or pet, do they interrupt their foraging and rise in retaliation with a low, even rattle.

These small but mighty birds are cavity nesters and compete viciously for favorite sites, even to the point of sometimes pecking competing bird species to death. More commonly, however, upon arriving on the breeding ground in May, males claim nesting territories by filling the available cavities, such as birdhouses and woodpecker holes, with thorny twigs. When the female arrives a few days later, she chooses her favorite from among all the cavities that her mate has claimed. She busily removes the twigs and builds a cup lined with grasses, fibers and feathers. Here she deposits five to eight glossy-brown, speckled eggs. They hatch in 13 days and the young flutter from the hole around 17 days later. House wrens nest twice in a season. After the young are reared for the year, House Wrens fall silent before departing in September for their winter home in the southern United States and Mexico.

Many people enjoy providing birdhouses for House Wrens. An entrance hole the size of a quarter is just right to accommodate these small birds yet exclude competitors.

## RUBY-CROWNED KINGLET
- ▶ distinguished from Golden-crowned by conspicuous eye ring
- ▶ small, slender bill
- ▶ stub-tailed
- ▶ ruby crown of male may be concealed
- ▶ hovers briefly; prefers conifers
- ▶ any kinglet without a crown patch and eye-stripe is this species

## GOLDEN-CROWNED KINGLET
- ▶ brightly striped head separates it from other tiny woodland birds
- ▶ female has yellow crown, male has orange, both bordered by black
- ▶ small, slender bill
- ▶ both kinglets flick their strongly-barred wings upward

# RUBY-CROWNED KINGLET
*Regulus calendula*

# GOLDEN-CROWNED KINGLET
*Regulus satrapa*

ext to hummingbirds, kinglets are our smallest birds. Ruby-crowned Kinglets are only four inches in length and weigh one-fourth ounce. Olive-green, with an eye-ring, wingbars, and a light edging to the wing feathers, Ruby-crowned Kinglets characteristically flick their wings as they hop among the branches. When capturing insects from the underside of leaves, they hover like hummingbirds. Only males possess the ruby crown that gives the species its name. The Ruby-crowned Kinglet's *tee-da-leet, tee-da-leet, tee-da-leet* song carries well considering their small size. Though they nest in the spruce and fir forests of northern New England, they are primarily known as spring and fall migrants through most of the East. Some individuals winter at lower elevations as far north as New Jersey. Seemingly fearless, they sometimes approach to within a few feet of people.

Golden-crowned Kinglets are slightly smaller than Ruby-crowned Kinglets. Like their "cousins," they are olive and have wingbars. However, they differ in having a white and black stripe above the eye. These stripes border a vivid yellow crown that in males has red in the middle. Their song is a complex series of rising notes followed by a descending *whip-lipalip*. Golden-crowned Kinglets are also insectivorous but less likely to hover than Ruby-crowned Kinglets. Though most associated with northern coniferous forests, the Golden-crowned Kinglet's breeding range also extends through much of New England and New York State. Scattered breeding populations are found through the higher elevations of the Appalachian Mountains as far south as North Carolina. Their nests, which typically hang as a mass of moss from a conifer branch, may contain up to ten white, spotted eggs. They nest twice each breeding season. Though migratory, Golden-crowed Kinglets spend the winter as far north as northern Maine. Despite their size, they are able to survive nighttime temperatures of minus 50 degrees Fahrenheit.

Ruby-crowned      Golden-crowned

# BLUE-GRAY GNATCATCHER
*Polioptila caerulea*

These lively, four-inch birds are nearly as tiny as their cousins, the kinglets. The "blue-gray" part of their name accurately describes their color, but their identity is cinched when one sees the white outer feathers of their comparatively long, black tails. They also have a light eye ring. The "gnatcatcher" part of their name is fitting because they prey on small insects such as gnats, as well as inchworms and spiders. Foraging birds can be picked out high in trees as they flutter and dangle among the outer foliage. Their high, thin *zeees* and nasal *mews* are constant as they work. These sounds are easily learned although too high-pitched to be heard by some people.

Blue-gray Gnatcatchers are most prevalent in the southeastern United States. They are mostly found at lower, warmer elevations south of a line from western New York State to Massachusetts. They are now scattered to Vermont and southern Maine, and there is evidence that their range is expanding northward. Because of their reliance on leaf-eating insects, they don't arrive on their breeding grounds until leaves have begun to emerge in spring. They winter along the Gulf Coast southward to Central America.

Most Blue-gray Gnatcatchers nest along deciduous woodland edges, especially near streams. Nesting commences soon after their return in April. Nests are saddled high on horizontal limbs. They are composed of spider webs, plant fibers, and down, resulting in an elasticity that enables the nest to expand as the young grow. It is camouflaged on the outside with bits of lichen. Despite their concealing features, nests can usually be located by following the activities of parents. Into these two-inch-diameter cups, the female lays four to five minuscule, speckled eggs. The young hatch in 13 days and leave the nest 12 to 15 days later. The earliest nesting pairs may nest a second time during the season.

**IDENTIFICATION TIPS**

▶ a bit larger than a sparrow

▶ male has bright, entirely blue back and rusty throat and breast (the Indigo Bunting is all blue below)

▶ appears round-shouldered when perched

▶ female is duller than male

▶ juvenile is speckle-breasted, grayish, but with some blue in wings and tail

♀

♂

# EASTERN BLUEBIRD

*Sialia sialis*

**B**luebirds are perhaps the most loved birds in North America. Their appeal stems from their delightful songs and perceived gentleness and tameness, but mostly for the vivid blue plumage of males. Male Eastern Bluebirds are brilliant blue on the head, back, wings, and tail, contrasting with a deep-orange breast. Females have grayish-blue on the body in place of the male's rich blue. Both sexes are about six-and-a-half inches in length.

The landscapes in which Eastern Bluebirds reside are nearly as charming as the birds themselves. They favor areas dominated by expanses of short grass with a few trees. Pastures, cemeteries, parks, and golf courses offer suitable habitat. They avoid wooded suburbs and forests. They were perhaps at their zenith in the eastern states when the region was dominated by small, diversified farms; they have retreated to an extent as vast areas have become reforested. Still, where habitat is appropriate, Eastern Bluebirds remain common and their *cheer-cheery-up* songs can be heard from March through August.

Eastern Bluebirds return to their breeding territories in March. Males defend their claims with song and, when required, skirmishes with competing bluebirds. If the conflict is with a neighboring pair, the female will assist her mate by entering the fray against the female of the opposing pair. Bluebirds are dependent on woodpecker holes and other existing cavities for nesting. Many people have discovered the pleasure of providing them man-made nest boxes. The popularity of this hobby is perhaps the reason that bluebird numbers have been increasing in recent decades. If constructed with a one-and-a-half inch diameter entrance, European Starlings, notorious competitors for nest sites, are unable to enter. Eastern Bluebirds lay four to six light blue eggs that hatch in two weeks. The young fly from the nest at 15 to 18 days of age. Bluebirds regularly nest twice a season, with young fledging in May and again in June. In the southern part of their range, where the breeding season is longer, they occasionally nest a third time in late summer.

The Eastern Bluebird's list of assets includes the fact that they are economically beneficial. Over half of their summertime diet consists of grasshoppers and crickets. Though migratory, a few winter as far north as Pennsylvania. The Eastern Bluebird's popularity resulted in their selection as the State Bird of New York and Missouri.

**IDENTIFICATION TIPS**

▶ Rusty head

▶ smaller than a Robin; plump

▶ distinguished from Brown Thrasher by round spots, dark eyes, and short tail; from other thrushes by the large round breast spots and deepening redness about the head

# WOOD THRUSH
*Hylocichla mustelina*

ere it not for their songs, Wood Thrushes would be inconspicuous residents of our forests and wooded lots. Luckily for us, however, they do sing and their glorious arias emanate from the interior of rich forests throughout the eastern half of the United States. Even well-forested suburban areas may accommodate a Wood Thrush or two. They are most vocal from late April through July, especially at dawn and dusk. Their songs are arguably the most beautiful of any North America bird. Their natural harmony is derived from the concurrent use of two vocal organs, resulting in flute-like notes that have a clear, almost ethereal quality. Songs are delivered in two-second phrases that end in delightful trills. These are repeated ten or more times a minute.

These birds of the woodland understory are rusty-brown above with conspicuously-spotted white breasts and white eye-rings. They are eight inches long. They feed on insects and other invertebrates on the forest floor. Having wintered from Mexico to South America, Wood Thrushes are back on their breeding territories between late April and early May. Nests are composed of grass, leaves, and mud, and are usually situated in the fork of a lateral branch within five feet of the ground. Eggs are glossy blue-green. A standard clutch contains three to four eggs. Incubation requires 13 days and the young fledge two weeks later. They nest twice each season.

Where forests are small and scattered, the nests of forest birds like Wood Thrushes are more easily found by Brown-headed Cowbirds. Wood Thrushes behave naively, usually accepting the cowbird eggs as their own and hatching and rearing the foster young at the expense of their own. This is perhaps the reason that Wood Thrush numbers are declining throughout much of their range.

# AMERICAN ROBIN
*Turdus migratorius*

obin "red-breasts" may very well be the best known birds in North America. Prevalent in yards and parks, they move quickly with a running skip, then stop abruptly to cock their heads. It has been suggested that they are listening for prey but they are more likely using one eye to watch for movement in the grass or at the surface of the soil. Robins especially relish earthworms, which they locate best in mown lawns and closely grazed pastures. They also eat various insects.

Today, American Robins range throughout almost all of North America. Two hundred years ago, however, before the advent of manicured lawns, they tended to be birds of the forest. But lawns and closely-grazed pastures provide such desirable habitat that their numbers increased and their range expanded. The introduction and spread of foreign earthworms may have also facilitated their range expansion because, in addition to using the worms themselves as food, they use the muddy worm castings to build nests.

Males, which have brighter breasts and darker upper-parts, claim territories from March through July with clear, liquid whistles and trills. If singing alone does not deter an interloper, a cock fight may ensue, culminating in the combatants thrashing about on the ground. Females alone construct the nests. Nests are built of mud and fine grasses, and are six inches across. They are usually situated in the fork of a tree, though occasionally on building ledges. There are typically four "robin's egg blue" eggs per clutch. It takes two weeks for the eggs to hatch and two more for the speckle-breasted young to leave the nest. Both parents feed the young. The first brood usually fledges in May or June and a second in June or July.

In winter, American Robins gather in flocks of up to a few hundred individuals that frequent woods, searching among the leaf litter for whatever insect remains they can find. They also eat the fruits of trees and shrubs. Highly nomadic, they avoid areas with prolonged snow cover and where the average January minimum temperature is below five degrees Fahrenheit. This usually places most of New England and the higher elevations of the Appalachian Mountains off limits. Elsewhere, people may see robins all winter and become amused at those who cite the first robin as a harbinger of spring.

The American Robin is the State Bird of Michigan and Wisconsin.

# GRAY CATBIRD
*Dumetella carolinensis*

**G**ray Catbirds were named for their mewing sounds, which are only a part of their highly diverse repertoire. They also emit squeaks, whines, and rasps, often as a rambling discourse during which the same sound is seldom heard twice in succession. Using both sides of its vocal apparatus independently, a single bird is capable of singing two very different songs at the same time. As if to further confuse an observer, Gray Catbirds incorporate the sounds of other birds from the neighborhood, and typically sing from the interior of a tree or bush so that an observer sees only a bit of the songster when it moves. Despite all of these challenges to identification, they are one of the easiest birds to identify because, taken together, these singing characteristics make them unique.

Gray Catbirds are charcoal gray all over with a black cap and a patch of rust below at the base of the tail. Their wings are rather short and a long tail attributes to their eight-inch length. The sexes are indistinguishable. Gray Catbirds eat a variety of insects and numerous small berries. Rarely, they can be attracted to feeding stations with cut-up oranges and other fruits.

Gray Catbirds winter along the Gulf Coast, in the Caribbean, and in Central America, and return to their nesting grounds from mid-April through May. They nest from the East Coast westward through the Rockies. They favor bushes and are commonly found in ornamental shrubs and hedges in yards. Nesting ensues soon after they return. Their bulky nests are typically well-hidden in thickets, briars, or dense trees. Commonly, four eggs are laid. They are glossy, greenish-blue, and hatch after 13 days of incubation. The young leave the nest 11 to 13 days later, usually in early June. A second nesting follows with the young fledging in July.

**IDENTIFICATION TIPS**
- ► white wing patches show clearly during flight; wingbeats are slow enough to be counted
- ► slimmer and longer-tailed than Robin; slender bill
- ► flicks tail from side to side

# NORTHERN MOCKINGBIRD

*Mimus polyglottos*

These familiar residents of yards and parks are renowned for their ability to mimic the songs of other birds. Tireless songsters, they sing nearly the year around and, during the full moon, even around the clock. They characteristically perch in the uppermost tip of a tree or bush and deliver a rapid-fire series of identical sounds before switching to an entirely different series. Snippets from birds such as robins, phoebes, cardinals, and quail might be incorporated into their songs along with whistles, *chats*, *mews*, and the occasional barking dog or squeaking gate. Listeners might be fooled briefly before realizing that the renditions are too rapid and repetitive to be real.

Despite their bewildering diversity, Northern Mockingbird songs apparently serve the same function as those of most songbirds: to attract mates and to defend territories from members of their own species. Prized territories contain berry bushes and are most strongly defended as the fruit sweetens, even in fall and winter. Known for their pugnacity, Northern Mockingbirds aggressively harass any animal that they consider a threat, including crows, cats, and sometimes, people.

Although the look-alike female also sings, the male is most vocal. When courting, he sings in flight. Males that encounter each other at territory boundaries perform a "boundary dance" in which they leap upward while flashing their white wing patches. Pairing occurs in fall, and nesting is underway as early as March. Nests are bulky, composed of thorny sticks, and hidden in trees, shrubs, or vines. Mockingbird eggs are brownish and blotched, and average four per clutch. The female alone incubates the eggs for the required 12 to 13 days. The stubby-tailed young leave the nest at 12 days of age. Mockingbirds nest a second time during the summer and newly fledged young may show up as late as August.

Northern Mockingbirds are most numerous in the southern states although, in recent decades, they have been increasing in numbers dramatically through New England. Their familiarity in the south has resulted in their selection as the State Bird of Arkansas, Mississippi, Tennessee, and Texas.

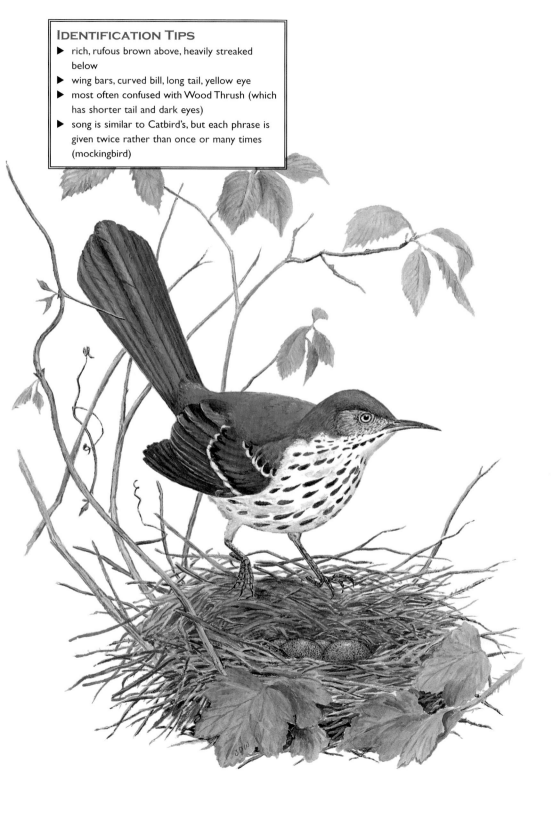

**IDENTIFICATION TIPS**

▶ rich, rufous brown above, heavily streaked below

▶ wing bars, curved bill, long tail, yellow eye

▶ most often confused with Wood Thrush (which has shorter tail and dark eyes)

▶ song is similar to Catbird's, but each phrase is given twice rather than once or many times (mockingbird)

# BROWN THRASHER

*Toxostoma rufum*

These long-tailed, rusty birds are usually seen flying short distances within a few feet of brushy cover along rural roads and in overgrown, brushy fields. Sometimes they visit suburban yards where hedges and ornamental bushes simulate shrubby rural habitat. Although Brown Thrashers resemble Wood Thrushes in appearance, they are separated by habitat, the latter being a bird of the forest. Additionally, Brown Thrashers are longer, half of their ten inches being tail, and have streaks versus spots on their breasts.

Like other mimic thrushes, such as Gray Catbirds and Northern Mockingbirds, Brown Thrashers are vocal with loud, diverse *squawks, peeps, mews,* and whistles. Though usually heard before seen because of the brushy cover in which they reside, Brown Thrashers are relatively easy to identify because of their unique songs. They tend to give the same phrase twice in succession. In contrast, Gray Catbirds sing one phrase then switch to another, and Northern Mockingbirds repeat a series.

Brown Thrashers eat beetles, other insects, and fruits such as blackberries, elderberries, and grapes. In winter, most retreat to the southeastern states, though a few individuals find favorable habitat along the coast to as far north as Massachusetts. During March and April, Brown Thrashers return to their breeding grounds, which extend throughout the East and the entire eastern two-thirds of the United States.

Singing and pairing commences immediately upon their return. Nests are usually well-hidden near the ground in bushes or vines. They are bulky structures composed of twigs. Brown Thrashers nest twice each breeding season, in April through May and June through July. First clutches typically consist of four eggs, second clutches, three. Nest construction requires about four days, incubation 13, and the nestling stage, another 12. The female alone incubates the glossy, red-speckled eggs. Both parents, which look alike, feed the young.

Following nesting, in August, Brown Thrashers become quiet as the new young strike out on their own and the adults molt into a fresh plumage. Brown Thrashers quietly depart for the South in September and October.

## IDENTIFICATION TIPS
- ▶ distinguished from blackbirds by its short tail and its browner wings (show best in flight)
- ▶ yellow bill is diagnostic in spring and summer; winter plumage is heavily speckled and bill is darker
- ▶ flies swiftly and directly, not rising and falling like most blackbirds

# EUROPEAN STARLING

*Sturnus vulgaris*

uropean Starlings are stout, six-inch birds that walk rather than hop. In flight, their wings appear translucent and a star-like silhouette results from the pointed combination of wings, head, and tail. For a few months following their annual fall molt, the black adults are speckled with tan and white. The speckles are actually light-colored feather tips. Through the year, they gradually wear off until by spring the birds are left with a black plumage that gleams green and lavender in various lights. Bills are yellow except in juveniles, which have dark bills and a uniformly brown plumage.

During their spring and summer breeding season, these gregarious birds emit assorted squeaks, trills, and rattles. They stuff their bulky nests into available holes, often in buildings. When using tree cavities, they may displace native hole-nesters, such as bluebirds. Their eggs are light blue and number four to six per clutch. Although their sharp bills are regularly used to take insects from lawns, these adaptable birds sometimes behave as swallows, catching insects high overhead. This is especially common in fall after the swallows have departed. In winter, they gather into immense, noisy flocks lining power lines.

European Starlings are so plentiful and widespread that it is difficult to believe that they are not native to North America. Their origin can be traced to 100 birds that were released in New York City's Central Park in 1890 and 1891. The organization involved was dedicated to the establishment of foreign birds in New York State and had successfully introduced House Sparrows 40 years earlier. A few years following their release, European Starlings began to expand their range westward. They reached Ohio by 1916, Missouri by 1929, and the Rocky Mountains by 1940. They now range from coast to coast, occupying such diverse habitats as city centers, farms, fields, and forests.

Their great versatility in nesting behavior and food habits contributed to their successful colonization of North America. In addition to fruits and seeds, European Starlings eat garbage, livestock feeds, and some crops. They also occasionally monopolize bird feeders, a problem that can usually be controlled by providing only sunflower seeds.

## IDENTIFICATION TIPS
▶ sleek, crested, brown bird with a yellowish belly; larger than a House Sparrow
▶ yellow band at the tail tip
▶ juvenile is grayer, softly streaked below
▶ fly in compact flocks; seldom seen alone
   except when nesting
▶ often indulge in fly-catching
▶ sexes similar

# CEDAR WAXWING

*Bombycilla cedrorum*

Through much of the year, Cedar Waxwings occur in foraging flocks of one hundred or more individuals. Relishing berries, they search them out whenever they are the sweetest and most succulent. Huge hackberry trees can be stripped of fruit in a matter of minutes by a horde of these energetic birds. Though classified as songbirds, Cedar Waxwings are incapable of producing anything resembling a song. Instead they emit tiny, buzzing *zeees* as they feed and fly about. This sound is usually the first clue that they are around. Upon looking up, an observer may be able to pick out an individual's pointed crest and the yellow tip of its tail. Binoculars are needed to witness the full beauty of these immaculate, six-inch birds. Their appealing features include a softly-hued plumage, black mask, and the startlingly red "wax droplets" on the wings that give them their name.

Cedar Waxwings live year round throughout most of North America. Flocks separate into pairs in June, July, and August to commence nesting. The extreme lateness of nesting is timed to match the ripening of the local fruit. In addition to berries, they catch flying insects, especially when feeding young. Nests are grass-made cups situated on horizontal limbs. Four to five gray, spotted eggs require 12 days of incubation. Another two weeks pass before the young fledge.

Nesting is seldom witnessed as compared to the conspicuous, nomadic flocks that invade neighborhoods to harvest the fruits of trees and shrubs. Favorites include cedars, dogwoods, cherries, hawthorns, crab-apples, hollies, and mulberries. Sometimes in spring, individuals become intoxicated on old berries that have become fermented by warming temperatures. They periodically collide with window panes, perhaps as a result of this affliction.

## IDENTIFICATION TIPS

▶ no other warbler is so thoroughly
   yellow; it's also the only yellow-breast-
   ed warbler that also has yellow tail
   spots (tail spots are white in others)
▶ no white in the plumage
▶ rusty breast streaks are more evident
   on the male
▶ female and young are told by the
   yellow tail spots

# YELLOW WARBLER

*Dendroica petechia*

 hough tiny, these flashy wood warblers readily catch the eye. Males are bright yellow except for olive upper-parts and streaks of rust on the breast. They have yellow wing bars and yellow tail spots. Females, such as the upper bird in the painting, are similarly colored though greatly toned-down. Courting males deliver a rapid series of six to ten clear notes that speed up toward the end, resembling *sweet sweet sweet sweeter than sweet*. Like other warblers, they glean insects and tiny caterpillars from leaves and twigs. Sometimes they hover briefly within foliage to take small flies.

Yellow Warblers winter in Central America and can be seen in every state as they move north with the emergence of leaves. They are only migrants in the most southern states. Their breeding range extends across the remainder of North America, north to the Arctic Circle. In the East, they nest from the southern reaches of the Appalachian Mountains northward through Maine. Throughout their breeding range, they associate with damp thickets, typically favoring willows. They sometimes visit yards offering similar habitat.

Nests are built in May, typically in the upright fork of a shrub or tree within ten feet of the ground. Favored damp thickets are sometimes occupied by several nesting pairs. Nests are three inches across and beautifully soft due to a composition of silky plant down. Commonly four to five eggs are laid. They are gray-white and wreathed with brownish blotches on the larger end. They hatch in 11 to 12 days, and the young depart the nest about ten days later. Yellow Warblers rarely nest more than once each year.

Unfortunately, these delightful wood warblers are one of the most common victims of Brown-headed Cowbirds. Those able to recognize the foreign egg proceed to build another nest directly on top of the previous one. Cowbird parasitism sometimes continues, resulting in as many as five tiers of Yellow Warbler nests with a warbler and cowbird egg in each tier.

**IDENTIFICATION TIPS**

▶ chestnut sides and yellow crown identify both
sexes in spring

▶ in fall, they are more lemon-greenish above,
white below, with some chestnut retained

▶ narrow white eye ring

▶ 2 pale yellow wing bars

# CHESTNUT-SIDED WARBLER

*Dendroica pensylvanica*

These four-and-a-quarter-inch birds are identified by the brown mark on their sides and their yellowish crown and back. Females have the same pattern but are less vivid. Males deliver a whistled song in spring and early summer that is described as *please please pleased to meetcha*. Chestnut-sided Warblers have responded favorably to human modifications of the landscape and are one of the most plentiful wood warblers in the northeast. They occupy the shrubs that grow where forests have been cleared, and are especially prevalent around abandoned farmsteads and along woodland borders of roads, parks, and campgrounds.

Their songs are mostly heard following their return from Central America in May. They are migrants through the entire eastern United States but settle in a breeding range that includes the higher elevations of the Appalachian Mountains and from Pennsylvania northward through all of New England. They also breed in the Great Lakes States and southern Canada. Nests are built in the shrubby understory within a foot or two of the ground. Chestnut-sided Warblers lay an average of four eggs per clutch. The eggs are white with brown speckles. They are incubated by the female and hatch in 12 days. The female alone broods the young, but the male helps to feed them during the ten-day period before they depart the nest. Chestnut-sided Warblers nest twice each breeding season.

**IDENTIFICATION TIPS**
- ▶ bright yellow rump, yellow patch on crown and on front of each wing
- ▶ spring male: blue-gray above, heavy black breast patch
- ▶ spring female: brownish, basic pattern similar
- ▶ winter: brownish above, whitish below, streaked, yellow rump
- ▶ also called "Myrtle" Warbler

# Yellow-rumped Warbler
*Dendroica coronata*

**O**f the nearly 40 wood warbler species that nest or migrate through eastern North America, Yellow-rumped Warblers are one of the most common and ubiquitous. Although only five inches in length, these active birds can often be glimpsed and identified among the foliage because of the vivid yellow spots on the male's shoulders, crown, and rump. The presence of white tail-spots, white wing-bars, and a black chest-band help to clarify the identification of these delightful blue-gray birds. Although much more subdued in color, females also possess the wing-bars and yellowish rump.

Yellow-rumped Warblers are relatively easy to detect because of their tendency during migration to forage in well-forested neighborhoods and in trees along the woodland edge. Where one is seen, there are usually a few others of both sexes. Perhaps the hardiest of warblers, a few winter as far north as Cape Cod in areas where there are over-wintering berries and active or dormant insects. They also follow Yellow-bellied Sapsuckers, feeding on the sap oozing from sap-wells that the woodpecker has created. It is during winter and migratory seasons that they are easiest to see because of the absence of greenery, a notorious hindrance to warbler-watching.

Yellow-rumped Warblers nest primarily in more wooded districts from the latitude of mid-Pennsylvania north through New York State and New England and west across Canada to Alaska. They arrive on breeding grounds in May, and observers can sometimes see them gleaning and fly-catching insects among the branches. They build their cup-shaped nest, typically on a horizontal branch near the trunk of an evergreen tree. They lay four to five white, brown-speckled eggs. The eggs hatch in 12 to 13 days and two weeks later, the young have flown from the nest. Following nesting, adults molt into the duller plumage that they wear until the following spring.

## BLACK-AND-WHITE WARBLER

- ▶ common in deciduous woods
- ▶ this and the Blackpoll Warbler are the only black and white warblers in the east
- ▶ white streak through the crown distinguishes it from the Blackpoll
- ▶ crown is striped in all plumages, but female lacks the black throat and cheeks
- ▶ feeds primarily along trunks and larger branches

## AMERICAN REDSTART

- ▶ active; flits about
- ▶ male is black with bright orange patches on wings and tail
- ▶ female is olive brown with yellow patches on wings and tail

# BLACK-AND-WHITE WARBLER
*Mniotilta varia*

# AMERICAN REDSTART
*Setophaga ruticilla*

American wood warblers are an incredibly diverse, large family, containing over 50 species in North America. Though all essentially the same size and shape, they differ in color and behavior. Many are yellow, in part, while others are blue, green, red, and orange. Black-and-white Warblers and American Redstarts are examples of the diversity among wood warblers in color, foraging strategies, and nest sites.

Though both species are insectivorous, Black-and-white Warblers typically obtain their food by creeping along branches and tree trunks, much like nuthatches. These four-and-a-half-inch birds occupy the forest mid-story. They breed through most of the forests of the eastern U.S., and across much of Canada, and like the American Redstart, winter in the Caribbean and Central America. Black-and-white Warblers return as early as late March. The male's courtship song is a rising and falling thin whistle repeated over and over. It is reminiscent of a squeaky wheel. Females are similar in appearance but lack the black throats and cheek patches of the males. They nest on the ground, laying four to five white eggs which hatch in 12 days. The young depart the nest 12 days later. Sometimes Black-and-white Warblers are confused with Blackpoll Warblers (*Dendroica striata*), which are also black and white. Blackpoll Warblers, however, have entirely black caps (not streaked) and white cheeks.

American Redstarts catch insects during short flights, very much like members of the flycatcher family. Males of this four-and-a-half-inch species are black above, white below (although their throats and upper breasts are black), and beautifully marked with orange patches on the sides, wings and tail. Olive-brown replaces black and light-yellow replaces orange on females; their entire undersides are whitish, including their throats. American Redstarts inhabit the forest understory, often near water. They breed from the East Coast nearly across the continent. Upon their arrival in April, their high *seet-seet-seet-seets* can be heard when in their habitat. They build nests in tree crotches. Their clutch size, incubation period, and rearing period are identical to the closely-related Black-and-white Warbler.

Black-and-white Warbler          American Redstart

**IDENTIFICATION TIPS**

▶ abundant in moist grassy or shrubby areas
▶ black mask distinguishes the male
▶ female and immature are olive-brown with bright yellow throat, buff-yellow breast; no black mask
▶ seen near or on the ground
▶ song repeated several times
▶ separated from similar warblers by whitish belly and brownish sides

♂

♀

# COMMON YELLOWTHROAT

*Geothlypis trichas*

f all the wood warblers in North America, Common Yellow-throats are the most numerous and easily seen. They are also the most peculiarly marked. Although females of this four-and-a-half-inch warbler are a simple drab-olive, males have black masks and vivid yellow throats that identify them with certainty. Seeing them can be difficult, however, because these are birds of the thicket. But the attentive birdwatcher can quite easily pick out their unique *which-ity which-ity which-ity* calls and then spot the little songster within the top of a clump of vegetation.

These continent-wide warblers favor the brushy countryside, especially where there is profuse, low vegetation in damp areas. Prime habitats are the brushy draws of pastures and the willows and reeds that border streams, lakes, and ponds. Careful observation may discern the little "bandits" flitting among the vegetation within a few feet of the ground. Common Yellowthroats eat small insects and spiders that they glean from vegetation.

Having wintered along the Gulf Coast and southward through the Caribbean and Central America, Common Yellowthroats return to their breeding range in late April. Nests are concealed near the ground and often composed of the same vegetation that supports them so that they blend with the surroundings. Three to five eggs constitute a clutch. They are a mere three-quarters inch in length, and white with speckles encircling the larger end. They hatch in 12 days; the young leave the nest in another 12. Both parents feed the growing young until they are totally independent at around 30 days of age. As with most warblers, there is only one nesting per season.

## SCARLET TANAGER

▶ male is flaming scarlet with jet black wings and tail (no other North American bird has a red body with black wings and tail); in July-August, red feathers are replaced with greenish ones; black wings remain

▶ first year males occasionally more orange than red

▶ female, immature, and winter male are a dull greenish above, yellowish below, with dark brown/black wings

# SCARLET TANAGER
*Piranga olivacea*

O ne of the most brilliant birds anywhere is the adult male Scarlet Tanager. His vivid red plumage, contrasting with black wings and tail, is a treat for the eyes, especially against a background of green leaves. Despite their brilliance, these six-inch birds are difficult to see because they tend to occupy the canopies of forests. Their songs are robin-like, but with a hoarseness. Their call note is a low *chip-burr*.

Females and juveniles are yellowish in place of red. Maturing males are blotched with red as they molt into adult plumage. Scarlet Tanagers return to their eastern North American breeding range around the end of April. Their nests are constructed by the females high in trees and rarely seen. A month-and-a-half is required to raise a family. They nest only once a season. Tanager nests are occasionally parasitized by Brown-headed Cowbirds despite their aggressive behavior towards these brood parasites. Scarlet Tanagers eat insects, small fruits, and occasionally, nectar from flowers. They can sometimes be attracted to cut-up citrus fruits placed out on deck railings, and they even visit hummingbird feeders.

Scarlet Tanagers depart for their wintering grounds in September. They winter with a multitude of tropical tanagers in Central and South America.

**IDENTIFICATION TIPS**
- ▶ smaller and more slender than a Robin
- ▶ head and upper parts black, rusty sides, white belly, long rounded tail with large white spots; female is similar but black areas are replaced with brown
- ▶ adult's iris is red; immature's is brown
- ▶ rummages noisily among dead leaves

♀

♂

# EASTERN TOWHEE

*Pipilo erythrophthalmus*

espite the snazzy plumage of the male, Eastern Towhees are more often heard than seen. Their rhythmic *drink-your-tee-ee-ee-ee-ee* songs emanate from rural woodland edges and brushy fields from April through July. Towhees are best observed by searching for these songsters amongst the foliage of trees or bushes. Brassy *chewink* calls reveal the locations of individuals hidden among brush and briars.

Upon sighting one of these seven-and-a-half-inch songbirds for the first time, the observer may notice the rusty color beneath and be reminded of an American Robin. But more careful observation will reveal that this color is only on the sides. Their former name, "Rufous-sided Towhee," is a fitting description of their appearance. The head, back, wings, and tail are black on males and brown on females. The tails of Eastern Towhees are relatively long and rounded, with white outer corners. Their flight is typically low and of short distance as they flutter from one hiding place to another.

Eastern Towhees range throughout the East between their arrival in April until their departure in late fall. Their breeding range extends westward to the Great Plains. Most Eastern Towhees retreat to the southeastern states in winter, but some can be found along the coast as far north as Maryland. They feed on beetles, millipedes, sow bugs, spiders, snails, and seeds. Food is uncovered by the peculiar method of scratching through leaves with both feet at once. People who are able to attract them to bird feeders may observe the same two-footed scratching technique beneath the feeder.

Eastern Towhees build bulky nests, well-hidden in bushes, either on or within a few feet of the ground. Their three to five cream-colored, speckled eggs hatch in 12 days and the young leave the nest by day ten, well before they can fly.

## FIELD SPARROW
▶ rusty cap; pink bill and legs
▶ clear breast
▶ less noticeable facial striping than other rusty-capped sparrows
▶ narrow, light eye-ring
▶ no dark eye line

**Field Sparrow**

**Chipping Sparrow**

## CHIPPING SPARROW
▶ bright rusty cap
▶ gray-breasted
▶ black line through the eye with a white line over it
▶ black bill and very white eye stripe distinguish it
▶ common on lawns

# FIELD SPARROW

*Spizella pusilla*

# CHIPPING SPARROW

*Spizella passerina*

ield Sparrows are rural birds, common in brushy pastures and scrublands throughout the East with the exception of northern Maine. They range west through the Great Plains. As is usual for sparrows, they are most often detected and identified by sound rather than sight. The Field Sparrow's song is a whistled trill that starts slowly and increases in rapidity with the rhythm of a dropped coin jingling to a stop. Visually, these five-inch birds are distinguished from most other sparrows by their pinkish bills, white eye-rings, unstreaked breasts, and rusty caps. Field Sparrows return from the southern states in March. Nests are five-inch diameter grass cups constructed near the ground in shrubs. Eggs are pale blue with a ring of reddish speckles on the larger end. They number three to four and hatch in 11 days. The young leave the nest 13 days later. Field Sparrows nest two or three times a season.

Chipping Sparrows are commonly seen hopping about lawns in residential areas and parks. At four-and-a-half inches in length, they are so tiny as to be half hidden in the grass. Identifying features include a dark bill, rusty cap, white eyeline, two white wing-bars and a plain breast. Their song is usually the first evidence of their presence, but most people would probably dismiss it as the sound of an insect. It is a high-pitched, rapid series of even chips, usually delivered from a low perch such as a fence or bush. Having wintered in the Gulf Coast states, they spread across the continent during April and nesting quickly ensues. Their four-inch diameter grass nests are typically situated in ornamental shrubs, hedges, or small trees, especially evergreens. Hair from pets, livestock, and even people is used as lining. Their tiny eggs are glossy-blue with black speckles on the larger end. A typical clutch of four eggs requires ten days of incubation, and the young fledge ten days later. As with Field Sparrows, Chipping Sparrows are regularly victimized by Brown-headed Cowbirds.

Field Sparrow    Chipping Sparrow

**IDENTIFICATION TIPS**
- ▶ heavily streaked breast with a large, central spot
- ▶ no yellow or buffy colors
- ▶ pumps its long, slightly rounded tail as it flies

# SONG SPARROW

*Melospiza melodia*

he most memorable aspect of Song Sparrows, as should be expected from their common and scientific names, is their song. They are more likely heard than seen and people who take the time to discern one bird sound from another are most likely to notice Song Sparrows. These six-inch birds are common and their trilling *maids-maids-maids - put on your teakettle-ettle-ettle* might be heard coming from brushy draws and streamside thickets from March through August. By keying in on the sound, the actual songster may be found, usually toward the top of a bush. They are recognized by their heavily streaked breasts with a spot in the middle.

Song Sparrows return to their nesting grounds in the northeastern states in March. Their breeding range extends on across the continent and north to the tree-line in Canada. Nests are typically well-hidden on or near the ground in thick vegetation. Their three to six eggs are pale green and heavily speckled. The eggs hatch in two weeks and the young leave the nest ten days later, a few days before being able to fly. Song Sparrows nest two to three times a breeding season.

Though they consume insects during the growing season, their diet switches to seeds and dried fruits in winter. They winter throughout all but the northern edge of the lower 48 states, and they would be inconspicuos at that season were it not for their tendency to form flocks. They sometimes visit bird feeders.

Though not shown, the Fox Sparrow (*Passerella iliaca*), another winter resident, is similar to the Song Sparrow in having a streaked breast with a spot at the center. They, however, are rustier in color and large for sparrows at six to seven inches in length. They often feed on the ground beneath bird feeders.

**WHITE-CROWNED SPARROW**
▶ pink or yellowish bill
▶ clear gray throat and breast
▶ puffy crown is prominently streaked with black and white
▶ shuns the woodland thickets that the White-throated Sparrow favors
▶ White-throated Sparrow is browner, has a well-defined white throat, yellow spot before the eye, black bill

White-crowned
Sparrow

White-throated
Sparrow

**WHITE-THROATED SPARROW**
▶ well-defined white throat
▶ yellow spot before the eye, black bill, short-necked posture
▶ seldom found far from dense cover
▶ usually feeds on the ground

# WHITE-CROWNED SPARROW
*Zonotrichia leucophrys*

# WHITE-THROATED SPARROW
*Zonotrichia albicollis*

These closely-related birds are large for sparrows, being nearly six inches in length. Their streaked heads and solid gray breasts distinguish them from other sparrows, at least when in adult, springtime breeding plumage. The main difference between them is explained by their names — White-throated Sparrows have white throats and White-crowned Sparrows have boldly black and white streaked crowns with prominent white centers. Fall and immature individuals have subtly streaked breasts and are generally more subdued.

In the East, White-throated Sparrows are the best known of the two species. They nest in Canada, New England, and upstate New York, and migrate through the region in spring and fall. Their song is especially easy to remember. It is a high, clear whistle with a slow cadence of *Oh Sweet Canada Canada Canada*. It can be heard the year around but the fall and winter version is sporadic and weak. White-throated Sparrows favor brushy woodlands. They nest on or near the ground at forest edges, and lay three to five brown eggs.

White-crowned Sparrows breed in the Canadian far north and through much of the western United States. They are seen in the East primarily during spring and fall as they pass through during migration, and are far less numerous than their "cousins." The White-crowned Sparrow's song also contains clear whistles, but it is more complex and buzzy. It is heard mainly on their journey back north in spring. Some of its song segments are inherited whereas others are picked up at a few months of age by listening to adults. Their noticeable regional dialects are probably the result of songs being learned from parents.

Both of these sparrows move about slowly and are easy to see. They flock with other sparrows during the non-breeding season, and often visit bird feeding stations where they favor the spillage on the ground.

White-crowned      White-throated

# DARK-EYED JUNCO
*Junco hyemalis*

These six-inch, immaculate, gray birds with the white bellies are most noticed in winter as they scatter from roadside brush, flashing their trademark white outer tail feathers. Males are darker gray than females, and first-winter young are streaked and washed with brown. Juncos visit bird feeders where they hop about, scratching and pecking at the spillage, favoring millet and cracked sunflower seeds. They also eat the seeds of weeds and grasses. These "snow birds" forage in loose flocks while emitting jingling twitters to keep in contact. Some individuals serve as sentinels while others concentrate on food-finding. These duties change off as they work their way through the underbrush.

Although ranging throughout the United States in winter, Dark-eyed Juncos also summer through a large portion of the East. Favoring cool, forested habitat, they nest from the tree-line in northern Canada southward through the higher, most forested districts of New England, New York, Pennsylvania, and down the Appalachian Mountains to as far as northern Georgia. They avoid low, flat, less forested landscapes. In the north, they associate with evergreens, and in the south, rhododendron thickets. Because they are birds of the woodland edge, they are often seen around mountain campgrounds.

Dark-eyed Juncos return to breeding territories in April and May. In contrast to their rather ground-dwelling behavior in winter, courting males select high perches from which to deliver their trilling courtship songs. They usually build their nests on the ground at the base of a tree, beside a log, or by hiding it in some other way. Their four to five eggs are glossy light-blue with a dense speckling of brown on the large end. They hatch in 12 days. Dark-eyed Juncos nest twice each breeding season.

Bird banding has indicated that, though breeding and wintering ranges are often separated by hundreds of miles, individuals are capable of finding their way back year after year to winter in precisely the same yard.

# NORTHERN CARDINAL

*Cardinalis cardinalis*

ale Northern Cardinals are one of the most splendid birds in North America. Sometimes it takes a visitor from abroad or from the western United States, where there are no cardinals, to remind us to appreciate them despite their commonness. Even the females, with their warm hues and reddish wings, tails, and topknots, are beautiful in their own subtle way. One of the noticeable features of these eight-inch birds is their heavy bill. These instruments enable them to crack almost any seed coat. They especially favor sunflower seeds. Cardinals visit sunflower bird feeders, particularly during snowy weather and even in the dim light of early morning and late evening.

The Northern Cardinal's song is as appealing as its appearance. It is a series of clear, loud whistles, often given from a neighborhood treetop. The repertoire is diverse, resulting in regional dialects and even songs that are suited for different habitats. Cardinals in deep forests sing slower and lower notes, apparently to enhance transmission. Careful listeners will notice that males near to each other will copy each other's songs, sometimes going so far as to sing duets. This apparently indicates a mutual respect for territory boundaries. Males and females sometimes sing together during courtship and nesting.

Northern Cardinals range through most of the East, though their numbers drop off in northern New England. Permanent residents, an individual may spend its entire life within a few acres. Nest building, typically low in a shrub, takes place in April and May. The two to five speckled eggs hatch in 12 days. The young leave the nest in ten days, when still too gray and stubby to be recognized as cardinals unless a parent is seen feeding them. They are able to fly well within a few days. Cardinals nest up to three times a season.

The extreme popularity of the Northern Cardinal is evidenced by it being selected State Bird by more states than any other bird: Illinois, Indiana, Ohio, Kentucky, North Carolina, Virginia, and West Virginia.

**IDENTIFICATION TIPS**

▶ rose bib of adult male is diagnostic

▶ thick, pale bill

▶ in flight, white flashes across the black upper plumage and rose wing linings are visible

▶ female is streaked, like a large sparrow or female purple finch; recognized by the large, thick bill, broad white wing bars, striped crown, and broad white eyebrow stripe; females wing linings are orange-yellow and conspicuous in flight

♂

♀

# ROSE-BREASTED GROSBEAK

*Pheucticus ludovicianus*

There are few events that provoke more excitement and curiosity among bird watchers than the first sighting of a Rose-breasted Grosbeak. Though fairly common, these attractive birds are only occasionally glimpsed. If a feeding station is operated in summer, that is the most likely place to see them. As with most birds, the males are the attention-getters. Their contrasting black and white coloration and rose bibs are splendid when seen against a background of green leaves. When in flight, a rose hue can be seen on the underside of the wings. The brown-streaked females are so different from the males that they might be mistaken for another species, unless it is noticed that they too are about eight inches long and have the same heavy, conical bills. These immense bills are used to crack tough shells and pods. They also eat buds, catkins, fruit, caterpillars, and moths. Their song is robin-like.

Rose-breasted Grosbeaks live in the eastern half of North America. After having wintered in South America, they migrate northward through the southeastern states in late April and May to their nesting ground, which extends throughout the East with the exception of the lower elevations of Virginia, West Virginia, and Maryland. Any wooded area is acceptable for nesting, whether a suburban yard or small woodlot. In the southern reaches of their breeding range, they favor woods along rivers or in other damp areas.

Nests are constructed of grass stems or twigs and are hidden among leaves in the fork of a tree or bush. A clutch contains three to six eggs, which are glossy blue and heavily blotched with purple and brown, mostly on the large end. The parents alternate in incubating the eggs. Both feed the young for the ten days that they are growing in the nest and for several days after they first fly. Although they usually nest only once a season, in the southern part of their range, where the nesting season is longer, they sometimes fit in a second brood. Rose-breasted Grosbeaks are frequent hosts to Brown-headed Cowbirds.

# INDIGO BUNTING

*Passerina cyanea*

These are the small, solid-blue, finch-sized birds that can be seen along woodland edges throughout the rural areas of the eastern United States. The solid-blue birds are the males, as females are a dusky brown. Males are so blue as to appear almost iridescent. Despite their abundance and brilliance, Indigo Buntings are not well known. Although they are among our most vocal birds, most people never notice them.

Beginning with their arrival in May, Indigo Buntings are heard almost constantly when in their habitat, even through the hot afternoons of July and August. The male's song is a strident ramble that rises and falls over a period of two to three seconds. Listening carefully, one can hear that most notes are paired. Though largely insectivorous, they also eat small seeds, berries, and buds. Males sometimes become so conflicted by the need to both eat and vocally defend their territories that they sing with food in their bills.

These four-and-a-half-inch songbirds are secretive when they choose, hiding among undergrowth and weedy tangles. Females especially adopt this habit when near their nests. Indigo Buntings nest twice during their summer stay. Females build a small, grass cup low in dense cover. They lay two to six glossy white eggs. Each nesting takes a little over a month. Brown-headed Cowbirds often lay their eggs in the nests of Indigo Buntings.

Like most songbirds, Indigo Buntings migrate at night. In a classic study of migration, those ready to depart Mexico's Yucatan Peninsula in spring were placed in cages in a planetarium in which a night sky was projected. Remarkably, most tried to fly against the side of the cage that faced the artificially created northern constellations, indicating that Indigo Buntings instinctively use celestial cues to determine the proper migration direction.

## IDENTIFICATION TIPS

▶ spring male is the only North America land
  bird that is solid black below and light above
▶ female and fall male resemble large sparrows,
  but have buff-colored crown stripes and
  breasts, and narrow pointed tail feathers
▶ female resembles the female Red-winged
  Blackbird, but doesn't have the Red-wing's
  heavy breast striping

# BOBOLINK

*Dolichonyx oryzivorus*

ompared to other birds, the coloration of Bobolinks is upside down, with the color on their backs and not on their breasts. Males of this seven-inch member of the blackbird family are black except for a patch of yellow on the back of the head and white markings on their shoulders and rump. Females, as well as males in fall, are entirely buff and, on the rare occasions that they come out of hiding and are seen, they are usually dismissed as some kind of sparrow. Bobolink males are most often detected by the bubbling songs they deliver while fluttering above the grassy fields selected for nesting.

There are few birds so limited to grasslands as Bobolinks. Not just any grass will do, however. It must be thick and at least two feet tall. Usually it must be several acres in size so that it will accommodate at least a small nesting colony. Damp meadows are especially favored, as are hayfields or oats with a component of clover or alfalfa.

Having wintered in the vast grasslands of Argentina, Bobolinks journey 5,000 miles northward in small flocks, arriving in the southeastern states in March and April. They quickly pass through this hot, humid region, spreading out to colonize suitable grasslands in the cooler, northern states from Maine to Oregon, usually during May. They nest sparingly through the lower elevations of Virginia and West Virginia, and commonly through all but the forested and urban areas from New York through New England. Although largely insectivorous, Bobolinks consume a variety of seeds, including grains such as oats and rice.

Nests are constructed on or near the ground in dense vegetation. Clutches average five to six eggs. Eggs are bronze with brown blotches and they hatch in 13 days. Each male may mate with one to several females. Occasionally, he will assist his primary mate with rearing the young while his secondary mates receive no assistance. The final egg in a clutch is laid a day after incubation begins so that it hatches a day later. This day-younger nestling can be sacrificed in situations where food is limited, such as for those females that do not receive male help. This increases the chance that the remaining young are reared successfully. To add confusion, however, it is known that the young in a female's nest may be fathered by different males. Young achieve flight in July. Bobolinks nest only once each year.

**IDENTIFICATION TIPS**
- ▶ male is all black with red and yellow shoulder stripes that are most conspicuous in spring (red is usually hidden during rest of the year)
- ▶ female is brownish with well-defined dark stripings below; they are longer billed and more heavily streaked than sparrows
- ▶ feed, fly, and roost in huge flocks

# RED-WINGED BLACKBIRD

*Agelaius phoeniceus*

ales of this widespread species are readily recognized by their red shoulder patches. These "epaulets" are easily seen when a male is in flight and, when perched, he displays them while delivering squawky *onk-a-ree* songs simultaneously with the slight spreading of wings and tail. When not behaving territorially, the shoulder coloration may be overlain with black feathers to the extent that only its yellow border shows. As compared to the nine-inch males, females are so small and brown-streaked as to resemble sparrows. Both sexes produce a *check-check-check* call while flying in flocks overhead or when their nests are approached too closely.

Red-winged Blackbirds are believed to be the most common birds in North America. This is surprising to most city dwellers until they realize that these blackbirds occur nearly throughout the continent and in rural habitats ranging from marshes to willow thickets to hayfields. In fact, Red-winged Blackbirds are one of the most likely birds to be seen along roadways during ordinary highway travel.

Males are first to return to breeding areas in spring, usually soon after ice has left the marshes that they favor. Those that are older and more experienced claim territories that are larger or have the greatest potential for nest sites and insect prey. Females arrive about a week later and, if a male has garnered an especially rich territory, up to eight may subdivide it and mate with him. Here they raise their young, typically with little help from the male, other than his defense of the nest from predators and other Red-wings.

Nests are composed of leaves and stems woven into upright vegetation such as cattails. They lay three to four eggs which are greenish-blue and scrawled with blacks and browns. The eggs hatch in 11 to 13 days and the stubby-tailed young flutter weakly from the nest 12 days later. A second clutch of eggs often utilizes the same nest.

Red-winged Blackbirds migrate to southern states in winter, although some find favorable spots in coastal lowlands as far north as Massachusetts. They form immense flocks during the non-nesting season. An estimated total of 20 million individuals was once recorded on a Christmas Bird Count in Missouri.

## EASTERN MEADOWLARK
► common in fields and on fences
► black V on bright yellow breast
► white outer feathers on short, wide tail show when bird is flushed
► several rapid wingbeats alternate with short glides

# EASTERN MEADOWLARK
*Sturnella magna*

These are birds of open grasslands. They are regularly seen perched on fences and utility lines, displaying yellow breasts and a black V-shaped bib on the chest. They are stocky, and about nine inches in length. When in flight, their short wings beat rapidly and they show the white outer feathers of their short tails. Due to their shape, short wings, and rapid wing beat, they resemble small quail. The Eastern Meadowlark's song is a high, slurred whistle that goes up and down the scale. They also emit a rattling call note.

Eastern Meadowlarks return to their nesting territories in March. They nest in hayfields, pastures, and road ditches from the East Coast west to mid-Kansas and central Minnesota. Grass nests are built directly on the ground and shielded with a roof of bent-over grasses. The female, who does all of the incubation and most of the feeding of the young, approaches and departs the nest secretly by walking along a hidden path through the grass. Her three to six eggs are white with dark speckles. They hatch in two weeks. They young leave the nest by 12 days of age, before being able to fly well. Meadowlarks usually nest twice each nesting season.

Eastern Meadowlarks eat insects, such as grasshoppers. Wintering individuals form flocks and subsist on weed seeds and waste grains. Wintering birds can be found as far north as western Pennsylvania and Massachusetts. Partially overlapping the western edge of the Eastern Meadowlark's range, in the Great Plains, is the range of the nearly identical appearing Western Meadowlark (*Sturnella neglecta*). Its range extends to the west coast. The Western Meadowlark has a delightfully bubbling song, which is probably the reason that it was selected as the State Bird of Kansas, Nebraska, North Dakota, Wyoming, Montana, and Oregon.

# COMMON GRACKLE

*Quiscalus quiscula*

These gleaming blackbirds with the long, keel-shaped tails are familiar to urban and rural residents alike. They are conspicuous in yards, parks, and along shores as they waddle about, searching the ground for such delicacies as worms, bugs, and bits of vegetation. Most people know them, but not by their official name, instead referring to them only as blackbirds.

Highly social, Common Grackles usually nest, travel, and forage in groups. Flock members sometimes threaten each other with the ritualized behavior of pointing their bills skyward. Or, they simply announce their presence with their familiar screeching squawk, delivered energetically with the simultaneous flaring of the wings and tail. When alarmed or to keep in contact with each other while flying about, they repeatedly emit *chack* calls. Seemingly intelligent, they learn by observation such behaviors as dipping food items into bird baths to soften them.

Common Grackles are one of spring's early arrivers and breeders. Up to 30 pairs will nest together in pine groves or dense foliage lining roads, streams, and lakes. Females, which are less glossy and slightly smaller than the 12-inch males, incubate the three to six pale green, brown-blotched eggs. The eggs hatch in about 13 days. Rearing requires another 12 to 15 days. Although silent around nesting colonies, the traffic of the busy parents can become so constant as to be noticed, especially during the latter part of the nesting period. Repeated flights into the trees bring food deliveries for the hungry young, while on outbound flights the parents carry small, white objects in their bills. These are fecal sacks that nestling songbirds commonly produce. They are dropped at a distance, presumably to lessen detection of the nests by predators. Common Grackles nest only once each year.

These well-known blackbirds breed from the East Coast west to the Rocky Mountains and well north into Canada. Following the nesting season, they gather into larger flocks, often with other kinds of blackbirds. The majority winter in the southern states.

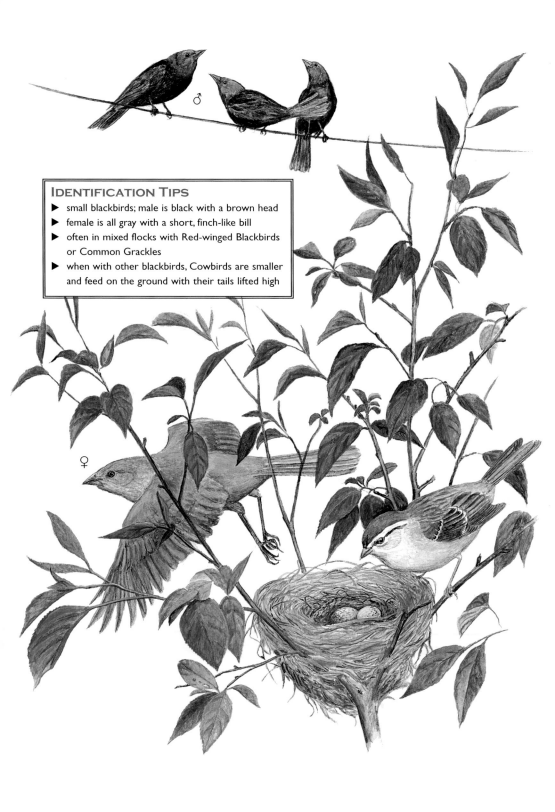

## IDENTIFICATION TIPS
▶ small blackbirds; male is black with a brown head
▶ female is all gray with a short, finch-like bill
▶ often in mixed flocks with Red-winged Blackbirds or Common Grackles
▶ when with other blackbirds, Cowbirds are smaller and feed on the ground with their tails lifted high

# BROWN-HEADED COWBIRD

*Molothrus ater*

These six-and-a-half inch birds live throughout most of North America in habitats ranging from forests to fields to towns and cities. Although traditionally in the company of cattle, there is hardly anywhere that one does not hear their squeaks and liquid gurgles or see a small band of the black, brown-headed males tilting and bill-raising to each other on an overhead perch. Cowbirds are easy to see, not only because they are common but because they tend to perch in the open. The drab, mouse-gray females especially use open perches to better observe potential hosts for their eggs when nearing egg-laying time. Egg laying can occur from March through August.

Most people are annoyed to learn that Brown-headed Cowbirds escape parental duties by fostering their young out to other birds. They are further disturbed to learn that the foster parents usually sacrifice their own young while unwittingly raising baby cowbirds. Brown-headed Cowbirds apparently evolved this remarkable behavior when following bison herds to feed on the associated insects and debris, thus abandoning the eggs that they had laid. Those eggs placed in the nests of other birds were sometimes raised and those cowbirds passed on refinements that caused the strategy to become even more successful. These included light-colored, speckled eggs that match those of many other birds, and smallish eggs to trick smallish birds. Brown-headed Cowbirds also produce more total eggs during the season so that they are able to parasitize a number of nests and thereby "hedge their bets." These eggs have a comparatively short incubation period so that they are likely to hatch sooner than the host's eggs. Also, Brown-headed Cowbirds tend to deposit their egg before the host's clutch is complete.

Originally more associated with the open prairies of the West, Brown-headed Cowbirds expanded their range to the East Coast by the late 1700s in response to forest clearing and the importation of cattle. This put them in contact with numerous bird species that were inexperienced with brood parasites and thus more vulnerable. Over 120 bird species are known to have been parasitized by Brown-headed Cowbirds, including the Chipping Sparrow shown here. Chipping Sparrows are examples of birds that occasionally raise one or two of their own nestlings in addition to the Brown-headed Cowbird chick.

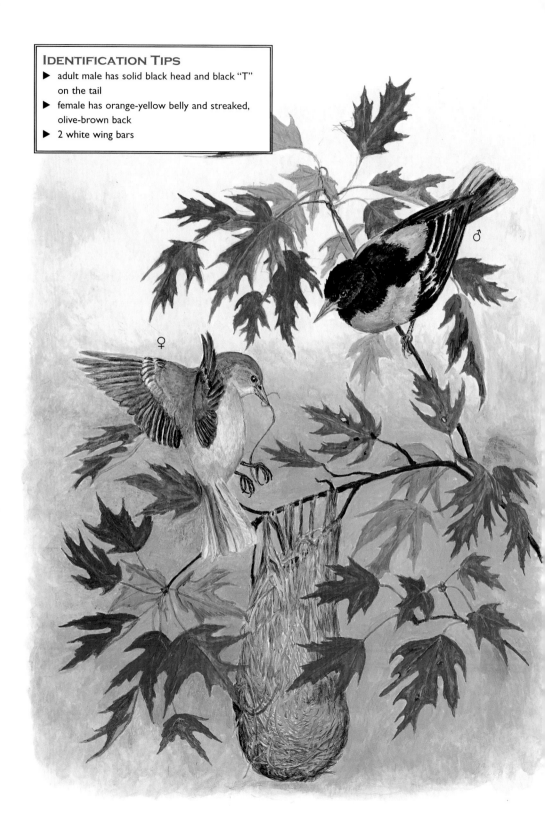

♂

♀

# BALTIMORE ORIOLE
*Icterus galbula*

hese seven-inch members of the Blackbird Family are among the most popular of birds. The dazzling males are known best. Females are subtly-colored and can be confused with other species unless one recognizes their similarity to males in shape, behavior, and habitat. Both sexes sing but it is the male's assortment of clear, flute-like whistles that especially attracts our attention. Both sexes emit a low chatter when disturbed.

Baltimore Orioles nest throughout the eastern states, though their numbers diminish somewhat in northern Maine. These are eastern birds, absent from the western half of the continent. They were well known to early settlers, who named them for Lord Baltimore, whose family colonized Maryland. The bright, orange and black feathers matched his family colors. Throughout the Baltimore Oriole's range, they favor tall trees along streams and in suburban yards. Because they glean insects from foliage, they wait until leaf-out before returning to their breeding range, typically in late April or early May, depending on the latitude. It is then that they begin courting and are most vocal.

These spectacular songbirds are perhaps best known for their hanging nests which are so intricate as to require up to a week of construction. Woven of grasses, strips of bark, stems, hair, and other fibers, nests are usually positioned high on the hanging tips of outer branches and so well hidden among leaves as to not be detected until after leaf fall. Sometimes several nests will be found within a few nearby trees. Some people delight in hanging out pieces of colored string that they later see woven into the nests.

A single clutch of four to five splotched eggs (pale gray to blue-white marked with dark colors) is produced each year. Incubation and the rearing of young requires about a month. Summering Baltimore Orioles will occasionally take "nectar" from hummingbird feeders and specially designed Oriole feeders. People can also attract them by putting out cut-up citrus and jelly.

Baltimore Orioles fall quiet during the heart of the nesting period. Like many other songbirds, they begin to sing again just before their departure in August. Over half of the year is spent on the wintering range which includes primarily Central America and Mexico, though some winter in the extreme southern U.S.

Fittingly, the Baltimore Oriole is the State Bird of Maryland.

**PURPLE FINCH IDENTIFICATION TIPS**

▶ sparrow sized; male is dull cranberry red and is more uniformly colored than other red finches
▶ female and immature are heavily striped; differentiated from sparrows by their heavier beaks, deeper tail notches, and undulating flight; differentiated from sparrows by the broad dark jaw stripe, broad light stripe behind the eye, and larger beak

♀
**Purple Finch**

**Purple Finch**
♂

♂
**House Finch**

**House Finch**
♀

**HOUSE FINCH IDENTIFICATION TIPS**

▶ smaller than Purple Finch
▶ male is brighter red than male Purple Finch, and red is more restricted to the head and back; also dark stripes on the sides and belly
▶ striped female is told from the female Purple Finch by its smaller bill and plain face (no eye stripe or dark mustache)

# PURPLE FINCH
*Carpodacus purpureus*

# HOUSE FINCH
*Carpodacus mexicanus*

These two closely-related finches are easily confused, both being about five inches in length and both having reddish-colored males and brownish females. The Male Purple Finch's red is slightly lavender, whereas the House Finch's is a shade towards orange. Purple Finch males may have faint streaking on their flanks, while House Finch males have noticeable brown streaking along their sides. Female Purple Finches are boldly streaked with a definite light streak behind the eye, whereas female House Finches are finely streaked with brown throughout. To further help in identification, the Purple Finch's tail-tip is notched, whereas the House Finch's is square.

House Finches remain in the region year round. Males mark the onset of the March nesting season with sweet warbling songs. Nests are made of fine grasses in such places as spruce trees, hanging flower pots, and decorative wreaths, where protected from wind and rain. They lay four to five pale blue, dark speckled eggs. The eggs hatch in two weeks and the young fledge two weeks later. House Finches nest two to three times a season, building a new nest each time.

Purple Finches usually nest in conifer trees. Their eggs, incubation, and rearing periods are essentially identical to the House Finch's. Though migratory, they nest throughout much of the East with the exception of lower elevations from New Jersey southward. Through the more southern states, they are better known as wintering birds, though they do nest in the higher elevations of the Appalachian Mountains.

Previous to the 1940s, House Finches were known only from the Rocky Mountains westward. However, because of their beautiful color and song, they were imported and sold in the east as caged pets under the name "Hollywood Finches." Some were released or escaped on Long Island, New York, in 1940. Within ten years, they began to expand outward from this beachhead in one of the most explosive range expansions ever documented. They had advanced to Philadelphia by 1955, Marlboro, Vermont, by 1968, and Buffalo, New York, by 1977. By 1990, they had expanded to their original western range.

Purple Finch          House Finch

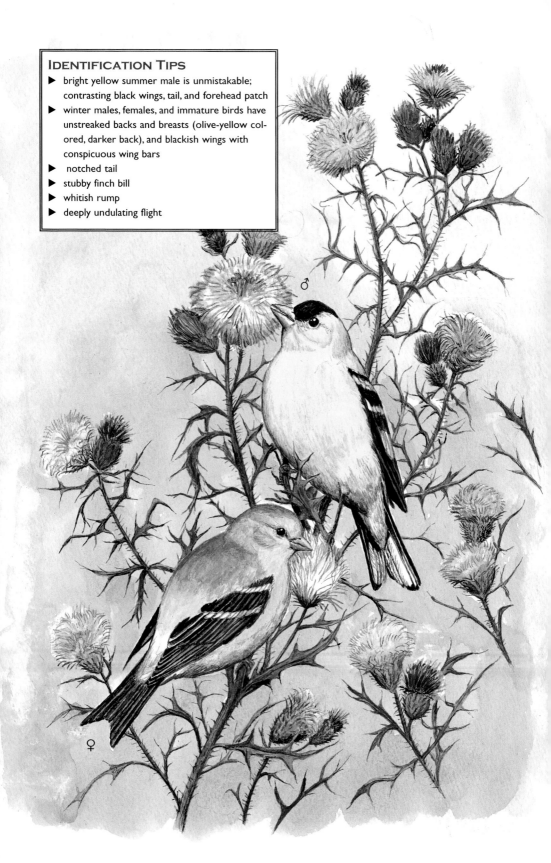

**IDENTIFICATION TIPS**

▶ bright yellow summer male is unmistakable; contrasting black wings, tail, and forehead patch
▶ winter males, females, and immature birds have unstreaked backs and breasts (olive-yellow colored, darker back), and blackish wings with conspicuous wing bars
▶ notched tail
▶ stubby finch bill
▶ whitish rump
▶ deeply undulating flight

# AMERICAN GOLDFINCH
*Carduelis tristis*

Thesese brilliant, four-and-a-half inch finches are common, especially in the countryside, from the Atlantic Coast westward across the continent. They especially associate with weedy fields over which they can be recognized by the repeated twittering that accompanies their looping, roller-coaster flight. If one is seen, there is usually at least one more, dipping and rising against the sky.

Sometimes called "wild canaries," males in breeding plumage are vivid yellow, contrasting with black wings and tails. Females are a muted yellowish-tan in place of the male's yellow as are winter-plumaged males. It is the duller-plumaged individuals that are most commonly seen because most people know them best in winter when flocks visit bird feeders. By mid-spring, soon after the males have began to brighten, they move to the country. Flocks may periodically re-invade towns, such as when dandelions go to seed, but most are afield from May through September.

American Goldfinches initiate nesting later in summer than any other of the Eastern States' birds. They pair off in spring, but most wait until July to build nests in synchrony with the ripening of thistle flowers. Thistle down is used to construct nests, while partially-digested thistle seeds are fed to young. Nesting habitat includes shrubby field borders and road ditches. Nests are typically situated within a few feet of the ground where a crotch is formed by four upright branches. The nests are only three inches across and so compactly constructed that they are reported to hold water. The miniature eggs are light-colored (bluish-white) and number four to six. The female builds the nest and incubates her eggs for the required two weeks. Both parents feed the nestlings for 12 to 14 days until fledging and for an additional three weeks following their departure from the nest.

The American Goldfinch is the State Bird of Iowa and Washington.

▶ male has black throat, white cheeks, chestnut nape, black bill

▶ females and young lack the black throat; have plain dingy breast and dull eye-stripe; streaked backs

# HOUSE SPARROW
*Passer domesticus*

These busy, five-inch birds are especially populous in cities, towns, and on farms. The male is recognized by his black bib, whereas the female is one of the plainest of birds. House Sparrows can become monotonous because of their commonness and their incessant chirping. They feed and nest in flocks and are most disliked for their habit of stuffing their grass and debris nests in the nooks and crannies of buildings.

House Sparrows are related to the weaver finches of Africa, a family that constructs bulky, woven nests of grass in trees. On the rare occasions that House Sparrow nests are built in trees, they somewhat resemble those of their relatives in being spherical with side entrances. The House Sparrow's four to six eggs are bluish and speckled with brown. They are commonly cushioned on a bed of feathers that the female has collected from the vicinity. The eggs hatch in 11 days and the young fly from the nest two weeks later. House Sparrows are nonmigratory, and they nest repeatedly from March through August.

Also known as "English Sparrows," House Sparrows are native to the Old World. Their origin in this country can be traced to introductions in Brooklyn, New York, and elsewhere in the early 1850s. Their subsequent expansion westward across North America was facilitated by the establishment of farms and towns. They reached the Mississippi River by 1870 and by 1900, they ranged from the East to West Coast.

It is thought that they similarly advanced westward through Europe with the advent of civilization between 7000 and 1000 BC. The domestication of livestock is believed responsible, as the little birds feed on the insects associated with horse manure. This relationship may explain why they were in greatest numbers in the United States around 1900, when horse use was very common.

In England, their populations have been mysteriously declining in many cities and farms during recent decades. In America, however, they remain fairly abundant because of their use of human structures for nesting, and because of their diverse food habits. They forage around fast food restaurants and picnic areas, and even glean insects from car grills in parking lots. Their association with humans has given them a "leg up" on native birds, such as bluebirds, with whom they sometimes compete for nesting sites.

# INDEX